BRICKS and ROLLERS

THE F...
PIONEERS ...

Zachariah Fairclough

BRIAN ESSAM

PAT FREEMAN

BRICKS and ROLLERS

Co-authored by
BRIAN ESSAM
PAT FREEMAN

ISBN 0 9523111 0 0

Typeset and printed by:
WICKFORD PRESS LTD
33 LONDON ROAD
WICKFORD, ESSEX SS12 0AW
Telephone: 0268 733212
Fax: 0268 561270

Published by the
EAST ANGLIAN TRACTION ENGINE CLUB
for the
EAST ANGLIAN TRACTION ENGINE SOCIETY
Registered Charity No. 296027

Other books published by the Club: THE OLD GUARD and THRESHERS YARD

"VAPOR OMNIA VINCIT"

MINNIE FAIRCLOUGH (left) and FRANK FAIRCLOUGH (who seems distinctly unhappy wearing a dress) twins of WILLIAM and CLARA, born 6th August 1901. Frank is now (1994) the oldest living Fairclough.

BRICKS AND ROLLERS

The Story of the Fairclouoghs of Clacton

ACKNOWLEDGEMENTS

To Co-Author Brian's wife Julie and children, Stuart, Cathy and Ben for supporting him during the research into this book. Also to Julie Fairclough and Janice Stapleton for the many hours of typing. Many thanks to Paul Howard and the staff of Cornerstone in Clacton for the invaluable use of "his/my" photocopier! But there is a special thank you to all the members of the Fairclough family who have reminisced and shared their memories. All those mentioned below have helped make this book possible. Please accept our apologies for anyone overlooked in these acknowledgements.

Clacton Library
Colchester Library
Public Record Office (Kew)
Essex Record Office (Colchester)
Essex Record Office (Chelmsford)
Essex Regiment Museum (Chelmsford)
Tendring District Council
Clacton Fire Brigade
Mr. & Mrs. Chapman (Filby, Gt. Yarmouth)
Mary and Late Freddy Wright
Adrian Corder-Birch
Mr. & Mrs. Leiper (Woodlands Farm)
John Taylor (Southend)
John Archer (Boston, USA)
Ken & Graham Austin
Roger White (Fire Engines)
Robin A. Harding
Late Alan Duke
Late Joan Topson
Late George Fairclough
Norman Jacobs
Mr. M. Catchpole
George Hardwick
Arthur Bullman
Roger Kennell
Hugh Perks
Theresa and Ray Cossey (Norwich)
D. J. M. Smith (Horse Drawn Carriages)
Kenneth Walker
Mr. C. Burcart
Frank Fairclough
Maude Fairclough
Rose Fairclough
George (Dennis) Fairclough
Jack Fairclough
Janet Fairclough
Elsie Haywood
Dick Harman
John Hooker
Ena Deans
Janet Mills
Gloria Lee
Susan Bollu
Margaret Bollu
Carol Caines
Gwen Gardner
Wesley Downes
Eddie French (Fire Brigade, Clacton)
Arthur L. Meek
Mick Baldry
Mary Fairhall
Trevor King
Steve Bullman
Peter Milton
Arthur Harman
June Freeman

Very many thanks are due to Adrian Corder-Birch, not only for providing most of the information on bricks and brick-making but also for his help in proof reading.

FOREWORD

by

ADRIAN CORDER-BIRCH, F.Inst.L.Ex., M.I.C.M.,

Hon. Auditor of the British Brick Society

It was a great honour and privilege to be invited to write this Foreword for Brian Essam and Pat Freeman's book, 'Bricks and Rollers–the story of the Faircloughs of Clacton'. This publication embraces some of my own interests; local and family history, the brick-making industry and the development of transportation.

This book is principally about the history of the Fairclough family during the last two hundred years and in particular the valuable contribution they made towards the expansion of Clacton-on-Sea. It is appropriate that the launch of this book will virtually coincide with a new road in Clacton being named after the Faircloughs. This decision by Tendring District Council illustrates the significant contribution which the family made to the town during the last 130 years. They had earlier lived and worked in other Essex towns and villages including Sible Hedingham, West Bergholt, White Colne, Earls Colne, Colchester and Walton-on-the-Naze. Many of them were brickmakers, latterly owning their own brickworks from where their business interests extended to builders, haulage contractors, road building and vehicle hire. The joint authors have carried out meticulous research into each of these occupations and those members of the Fairclough family associated with them. Some excellent illustrations adorn the text showing members of the family and the various activities with which they were involved. A variety of amusing anecdotes and memories have been included which will all contribute to the enjoyment of readers.

The authors have compiled an excellent book drawing upon their respective areas of knowledge. Brian Essam is related to the Fairclough family by marriage and Pat Freeman is an authority on steam rollers which feature prominently in this volume.

This is a very enthralling and informative family history which I thoroughly commend to you.

Adrian Corder-Birch

May 1994

ADRIAN CORDER-BIRCH

The Maltings, North End Road, Little Yeldham, Halstead, Essex CO9 4LE.

INTRODUCTION

Julie Essam, wife of co-author Brian, was born a Fairclough and this fact provided the spur to investigate the history of one of Clacton's oldest families. Local history books mention people such as J. Harman, J. Agate, W. P. Jackson, H. J. Page, A. Penfold and Peter Bruff as leading lights in the evolution of Clacton, but it would appear that the contribution of the Fairclough's has largely been overlooked. We believe that they played a very important part in the growth of Clacton and we hope that this book will go some way towards setting the record straight.

It may seem somewhat odd that we should have chosen "Bricks and Rollers" as the title for this book but we believe it to be very relevant to the story.

Bricks, to most people, are mundane objects but they loom large in the annals of the Faircloughs. Not only were some of them involved in brick production and supply, for example for the Colne Valley and Halstead Railway and the Tendring Hundred Railway construction, but later on Zachariah Fairclough, who is central to this story, used an enormous number of them when building a large proportion of houses in Clacton and surrounding areas.

Zachariah was also involved in the construction of most of Clacton's early roads and his Steam Rollers played an essential part in this work and they were also contracted out to local authorities in Colchester, Dovercourt and surrounding districts.

However, besides bricks and rollers, many other subjects are pertinent to the Fairclough story and these we have detailed at some length as well as giving some relevant anecdotes.

Suffice it to say that we hope this book will be seen as not just a record of the Faircloughs but that it mirrors other unsung pioneering families and their contribution to the evolution of local history in many parts of the country.

BRIAN ESSAM
PAT FREEMAN

Family Origins

"Fair of face, pretty and dwellers of the valley or ravine" is a given meaning of the name of Fairclough of which there are several spelling variations, two of which are Ffairclough and Faircloth.

It may be fanciful to believe that the Fairclough of East Anglia originated from Simon de Ffairclough, who held sway in 1332, but it is a definite fact that their family tree can be traced from 1793 onward.

On the 19th November of that year it is recorded that William Faircloth married Rebecca Fincham in Sible Hedingham, Essex. The issue from this marriage was two sons and two daughters, of which the salient one, for the purpose of this story, was Thomas Faircloth who was born on 6th May 1798. It is interesting to note that at some stage his name changed to Fairclough (still pronounced Faircloth) as it had for his brother whilst his two sisters still retained the name of Faircloth.

On 23rd October 1820 Thomas married Charlotte Howe and in 1827 William was born who becomes even more central to this family history.

This is an appropriate place to write a few words about the construction of two railway branch lines as they are both very relevant to the life story of the Fairclough.

East Anglian Branch Lines

The growth of the railway system during the last century was mainly responsible for the stimulation of trade in this country by providing easier access from remote areas to centres of consumption and distribution.

Around the middle of that century businessmen either side of Colchester, Britain's oldest recorded town, realised this fact and saw the need for railway branch lines to connect up to Colchester and thereon to London. The upshot was the eventual construction of the Colne Valley Railway to the west and the Tendring Hundred Railway to the east of Colchester.

On 30 June 1856, an application by the Colne Valley and Halstead Railway company to construct a line from Chappel (where the junction was to be with the Stour Valley Railway) to Halstead was approved by Parliament and on 13th August 1859, a further Act authorised the company to extend the line from Halstead to Haverhill. Work commenced in February 1858 and the line Chappel to Halstead was completed in April 1860. The section from Halstead to Castle Hedingham was opened in July 1861, that to Yeldham in May 1862 and the final section to Haverhill in May 1863.

On 13th July 1863, an Act of Parliament authorised the Tendring Hundred Railway Company to build a line from Wivenhoe (the existing branch line from Colchester), to Walton-on-the-Naze, via Alresford, Thorington, Great Bentley, Weeley, Thorpe-le-Soken and Kirby Cross. This line was opened in stages: to Weeley in January 1866, to Kirby Cross in July 1866 and to Walton in May 1867.

From Clacton's point of view, this was not a satisfactory state of affairs as visitors using the railway had to rely on the services of a stage coach meeting each train at Weeley to get them to this embryo seaside resort.

In August 1877, the Clacton Railway obtained an Act which authorised them to construct a spur line from Thorpe-le-Soken to Clacton and work started in July 1878 but, due to unforeseen difficulties, was not finished until July 1882.

Construction of these railways therefore spanned a total of 24 years (1858-1882). This provided much needed work for local people, not least for those employed in brickfields who were called upon to provide the millions of bricks needed to build new station complexes and bridges.

The map on Page 10 shows the position of known brickworks in relation to stations along both lines and the probability is that bricks from many of these fields were used in their construction.

Typically it is known that a brickworks at White Colne, located to the rear of White Colne chapel, definitely did provide bricks for the Colne Valley Railway and that the brickyard was cleared and the kiln demolished about 1861 or 1862 just a year or two after the line was opened to White Colne and Earls Colne stations.

Similarly it is on record that a brick kiln within one mile of Sible Hedingham also provided bricks for the Colne Valley line. The station there was opened for traffic in 1861 and the brick kiln, materials and tools were for sale by auction on 14th October 1862.

To enable the reader to identify more closely with the Faircloughs who were, for a great many years, closely associated with the brick making industry, there follows a description of the configuration and operation of a typical 19th century East Anglian Brickfield.

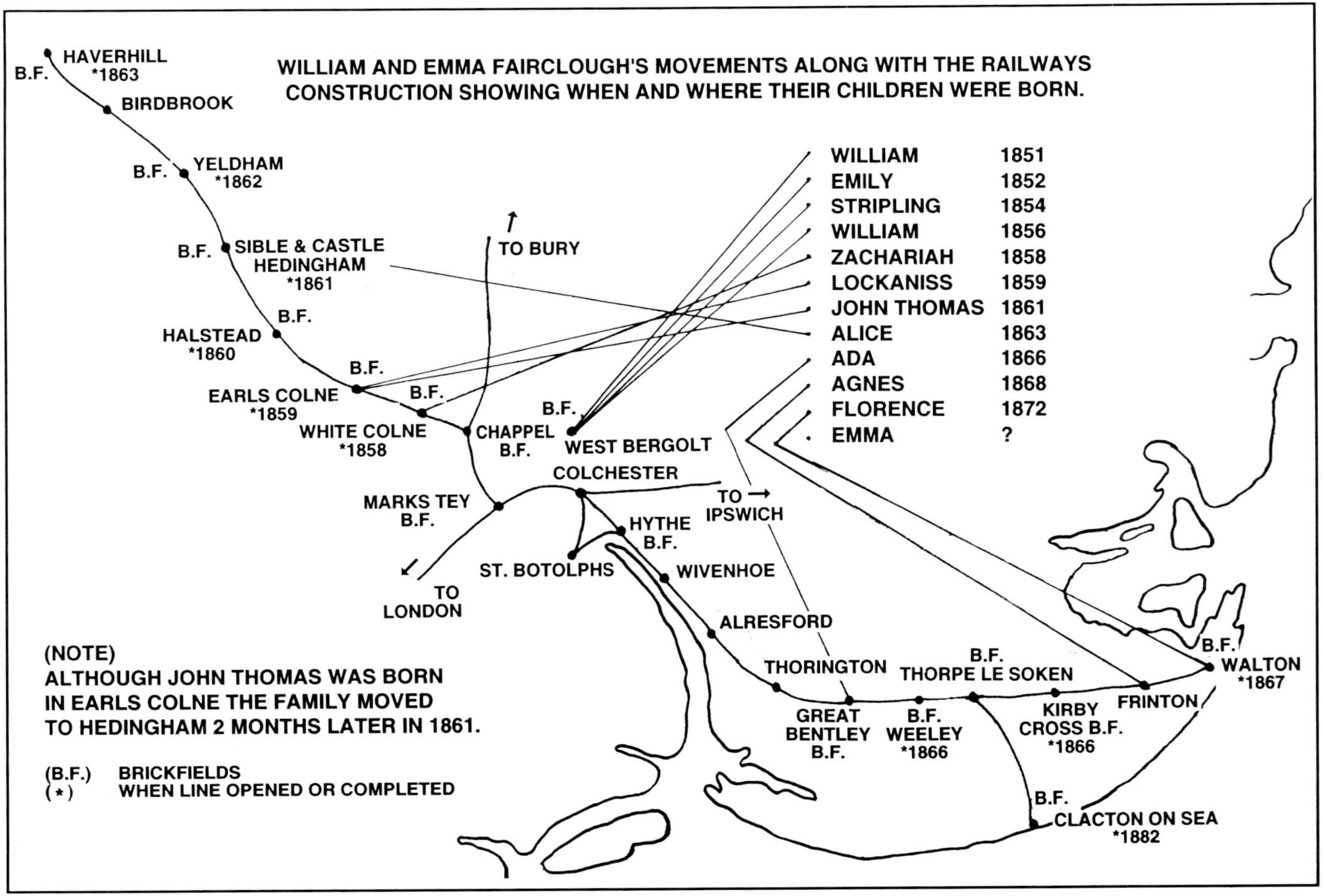
WILLIAM AND EMMA FAIRCLOUGH'S MOVEMENTS ALONG WITH THE RAILWAYS
CONSTRUCTION SHOWING WHEN AND WHERE THEIR CHILDREN WERE BORN.
WILLIAM 1851
EMILY 1852
STRIPLING 1854
WILLIAM 1856
ZACHARIAH 1858
LOCKANISS 1859
JOHN THOMAS 1861
ALICE 1863
ADA 1866
AGNES 1868
FLORENCE 1872
EMMA ?
B.F. HAVERHILL *1863
BIRDBROOK
B.F. YELDHAM *1862
B.F. SIBLE & CASTLE HEDINGHAM *1861
B.F. HALSTEAD *1860
B.F. EARLS COLNE *1859
B.F. WHITE COLNE *1858
CHAPPEL B.F.
TO BURY
B.F. WEST BERGOLT
COLCHESTER
MARKS TEY B.F.
TO LONDON
TO IPSWICH
HYTHE B.F.
ST. BOTOLPHS
WIVENHOE
ALRESFORD
THORINGTON
GREAT BENTLEY B.F.
B.F. WEELEY *1866
B.F. THORPE LE SOKEN
KIRBY CROSS B.F. *1866
FRINTON
B.F. WALTON *1867
B.F. CLACTON ON SEA *1882
(NOTE)
ALTHOUGH JOHN THOMAS WAS BORN
IN EARLS COLNE THE FAMILY MOVED
TO HEDINGHAM 2 MONTHS LATER IN 1861.
(B.F.) BRICKFIELDS
(*) WHEN LINE OPENED OR COMPLETED

Bricks and Brickmaking

"... Let us make brick, and burn them thoroughly. And they had brick for stone and slime they had for mortar" (slime was bitumen).

That is probably the earliest written record of the use of brick, appearing as it does in the Bible (Genesis, Chapter XI v3) in connection with the projected building of the Tower of Babel over 4000 years ago.

However, it is known that sun dried bricks were used in Middle Eastern countries as long ago as 9000 BC and brick must, therefore, rank as the oldest manufactured building material.

Brickmaking was probably introduced into England by the Romans well before the end of the first century, but after they left this country very little (if any) brickmaking was carried out until the last half of the 12th century. Then, due probably to trading connections with the Netherlands, the industry revived and during the late Medieval and Tudor periods brickmaking expanded in East Anglia. This was no doubt due to increased prosperity with consequent improvement in housing standards and the population explosion in the aftermath of the Industrial Revolution was probably responsible for the steady growth of the industry as can be gauged by the census records, for Essex, of persons engaged in brickmaking during the 19th century as follows:-

1831	388	**1891**	1,207
1871	860	**1901**	2,136

During the 20th century there has been an equally steady decrease in the number of brickmakers in Essex.

It is interesting to note that a large majority of parishes had a brickfield at one time or another and though the physical evidence may have long ago disappeared a variety of names still exists to give an indication of their previous locations. Such names often started with a word, or words, connected to brickmaking such as Brick Kiln, Clamp, Clay, Clay Pit, Kiln, Kiln Croft, Pot Kiln, Pot Croft, Potters or Tile, followed by, for example, Pastures, Meadows, Field, Place, Hill or Croft.

Brickmaking (Hand Made)

Clay for the bricks was dug by hand during the winter months and was left in a heap so that the frost, rain and sun could break it up. In the spring, when all risk of frost had passed, (very cold weather could damage 'green' bricks), the clay was made ready for the brickmaker. If it contained stones it was either discarded or put through a 'wash mill' where the stones were filtered out, but if it was stone free it was put through a 'pug' mill. This was a large, circular, stationary container about two metres high and one metre in diameter, which had a central vertical shaft attached to which were a number of horizontal knives. Clay was put into the top and as this shaft was rotated, the knives cut and mixed it. Water was added during this process to bring the clay to the right consistency and eventually it was forced through the opposite end of the mill where it was in a suitable condition for the brickmakers. Pug mills were initially powered by a horse, or pony, harnessed to a long beam which was attached to the centre shaft of the mill around which the animal endlessly circled.

Photo: Adrian Corder-Birch collection

BEACH'S Brickworks, Chelmsford, c.1900. The horse is driving the Pug mill. A cradle barrow is loaded with 'green' bricks ready to be wheeled to the drying sheds.

Later, steam engines, then internal combustion engines, were used to perform this 'pugging'. As the clay was forced out of the bottom of the pug mill, a labourer, or 'temporer', picked up the pug, as it was known at that stage of the operation, and put it on the brickmakers table. To pick up the pug the temporer used a 'cockle' which was an implement that cut easily through the pug and which could be used to lift it onto the table without sticking. Fixed to the table was a stockboard over which the mould, a wooden frame with no top or bottom, was placed. If a 'frog', or indent, was required in the brick, a piece of wood the inverse shape of the frog was attached to the stockboard.

The actual making of the brick was then carried out. The mould and stockboard were either sanded or wetted to prevent clay adhering, then the brickmaker took a 'warp' or 'clot' of the pug, raised it above his head, and with great force threw it down into the mould ensuring that it was completely filled right into the corners. He then pulled a 'strike' across the top of the mould to remove the surplus clay. The resulting 'green brick' was removed in its mould and placed on a pallet board which was larger in area than the brick. The mould was then removed by slipping it upwards leaving the green brick on the pallet board and it was then transferred to a cradle or hack barrow.

In the foreground is the mould which is placed over the stockboard (rear). Both of these come from the Coopers Lane brickworks and were given to ARTHUR HARMAN by WILLIAM FAIRCLOUGH.

Photo: Brian Essam

Cradle barrows were special long wheelbarrows with springs to minimise vibration as great care had to be taken in handling the green bricks as they had no mould to protect them. When fully loaded with about 30 bricks, a 'bearer off' (or pusher-out), wheeled it to the 'hacks' (derived from hackstead–a place for drying green bricks), which were rows of long low drying sheds consisting of a roof with no sides. The bricks were then carefully removed from the barrow and were placed in the hack, on their sides about an inch apart at an angle to the hacks and the next course of bricks was placed at an opposite angle (when the first course was partly dry), thus allowing the sun and wind to dry the bricks. After a few days, these green bricks were 'scintled', that is to say they were turned round the opposite way so that the other surfaces could dry out. The bricks in the hacks were laid in two rows up to eight courses high and the process took up to six weeks, depending upon the type of weather.

At this stage, the bricks were, in effect, just lumps of dried clay and to change them into finished bricks they had to be burnt at bright red heat (around 1000°C) and there were two methods of doing this–clamp and kiln. Burning by the clamp process saved the considerable cost of constructing a kiln and was often used when brickmaking was carried out periodically and was close to the building under construction.

Photo: Brian Essam

Key to the drying shed at Coopers Lane Brickworks, owned by DICK HARMAN.

The kiln was a permanent structure, generally sited where the basic material, clay, was available in large quantities and where transport was readily available to enable bricks to be distributed over a wide area.

The process of burning in clamps took a few weeks and in kilns four days and the outcome was, in both cases, an item of building material that was virtually indestructible. As mentioned earlier, brickmaking was a seasonal trade which meant that most employees were 'laid off' during the winter months which must have been a great hardship for a married man when there was no unemployment pay. As brickmakers were generally paid piecework, they had to work flat out during the spring, summer and autumn to earn enough to see them through the winter. To achieve a high throughput of bricks the brickmaker often enlisted the help of his family, although they would not receive any direct pay. It was not, therefore, uncommon for the wife to help with the making of the bricks and the children to act as labourers. They would put the pug onto the table and remove the green bricks onto a cradle barrow. An adult, usually the wife, would wheel the loaded barrow to the hacks and leave it there to be unloaded and returned by the children, who would then stack and 'scintle' the bricks. It was known that children as young as seven years of age were 'employed' in this manner, but during the last century it must have been 'all hands to the pump' for the family to survive.

Photo: Adrian Corder-Birch collection

FRED CORDER (left) 1885-1961 and his brother HARRY 1873-1942, standing in front of an updraught kiln at the SOUTHEY GREEN BRICK, TILE & POTTERY WORKS, SOUTHEY GREEN, SIBLE HEDINGHAM, which was owned by the CORDER family from 1859 to 1942. This was one of the only two brickworks in the village c.1861 when WILLIAM FAIRCLOUGH was working along the railway. Photo taken c.1931.

Brick Transport

Until the introduction of branch line railways into East Anglia, brick transport from local brickfields was mainly done by horse and cart and specialist vehicles were used, pulled by two horses that could carry about 800 bricks. However, due to the bad state of existing roads it was found more expedient when long distances were involved to float the bricks. One such brickworks which used this method was at Ballingdon Grove, near Sudbury owned by R. A. Allen. He had a special channel cut from his brickworks to connect with the nearby Stour River and used barges which could transport about 26 tons of bricks. They were usually worked in pairs pulled by horses until, in about 1864, the first steam barges appeared. The laden barges travelled down the Stour on their way to London where bricks were in great demand and it is interesting to note that Ballingdon bricks were used to build the Albert Hall and Kensington Museum.

Another method of transport was to use steam traction engines to haul substantial loads of bricks. One of their drawbacks however, was that their heavy weight and that of the load could easily spoil the surface of the roads.

With the advent of the internal combustion engine, lorries soon took over brick transportation with the subsequent decline in the use of horse and carts, barges and traction engines.

Photo: Adrian Corder-Birch collection

Two loaded barges being towed by a horse along the STOUR river near WORMINGFORD– pre First World War.

Photo: Hugh Perks collection

Bricks being unloaded from barges at Clacton.

Photo: Adrian Corder-Birch collection

Bricks being loaded onto a barge c.1905. The barges at BALLINGDON would have been loaded like this.

Photo: Adrian Corder-Birch collection

This Traction Engine, owned by the Rev. BASIL J. H. BERIDGE, was used for hauling bricks from his brickworks in Halstead. Here it has crashed into the wall of ST. ANDREW'S Churchyard, HALSTEAD, in May 1903.

The coming of the railways into the area meant that many bricks were carried by this method and indeed, extra trains were required to cope with the expanding brick production. One such was Locomotive No. 5 (0-6-2T), purchased by the Colne Valley and Halstead Railway in 1908, particularly to be used for the brick trade at Hedingham. It is also interesting to note that some brickfields had their own private sidings which cut out the need for intermediate handling of the bricks and therefore, facilitated and speeded up their transportation. Sible and Castle Hedingham and Haverhill along the Colne Valley Line were known to have had their own sidings. However, it was only when researching for this book that it was discovered that there had been a brickfield at Thorpe, on the Tendring Hundred Line, and it also had its own siding. What is more, the route of the siding can still be clearly seen and it leads to the remains of the kiln, parts of which are still standing (see Appendix 3).

Photo: Adrian Corder-Birch collection

Loco No. 5 of the COLNE VALLEY & HALSTEAD Railway entering HALSTEAD Station with the 12.20 p.m. HAVERHILL to CHAPPEL goods train on 6th August 1909. This 'up' goods train includes several trucks of bricks from PURLS HILL siding, SIBLE HEDINGHAM, where the HEDINGHAM BRICK Coy. was situated.

Photo: Adrian Corder-Birch collection

Loading bricks onto trucks at the HEDINGHAM BRICK & TILE work siding from the COLNE VALLEY & HALSTEAD railway line, about 1895. The man in the bowler hat is DAVID CORNISH manager of the brickworks for the proprietor MARK GENTRY. JOHN CORDER (1863-1957) who was burner of the bricks for over 50 years, until he retired aged 75, is on the top of the kiln and his eldest son, Edward, is the young boy standing on the left. This view shows the 'updraught' kilns and kiln barrows.

William Fairclough (1827 - 1889)

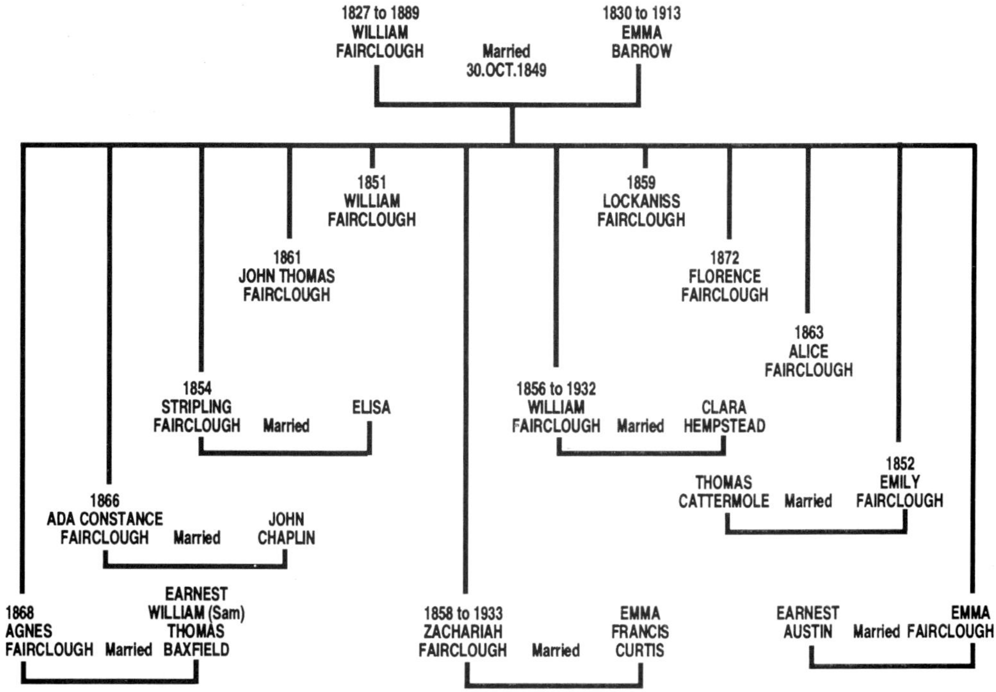

William, the second son of Thomas and Charlotte Fairclough, was born at West Bergholt, Essex in 1827. In the 1841 census it is recorded that he was still there, living with his parents and both he and his father were employed as agricultural labourers. On 30th October 1849, he married the 'girl next door', Emma Barrow, and by the time the 1851 census was taken in West Bergholt he was employed as a 'Brickmaker' and had a son, William (who unfortunately died soon afterwards).

Whether by design or circumstance, William had chosen a trade which was to provide him and his family with a guaranteed living right up to his death on 27th November 1889. The 1861 census shows that William and Emma were living at Sible Hedingham in Mill Lane (now known as Alderford Street), together with their five children Emily, Stripling and William, all born at West Bergholt, Zachariah born at White Colne and John Thomas born at Earls Colne. A further son Lockaniss had been born at White Colne in 1859, but must have died before the 1861 census took place.

The next census, in 1871, established that William and Emma were living in Frinton Road, Kirby, together with two more daughters, Ada born in Great Bentley and Agnes born at Frinton. Another daughter, Florence, was born in 1872 at Walton.

The location of brickfields, the places and dates of birth of the children and the opening times of various sections of the Colne Valley Railway and the Tendring Hundred Railway (see map on Page 10) demonstrates quite clearly that William and Emma and family moved along the lines as they were being constructed. It seems obvious that William was involved in the provision of some of the millions of bricks which these two railways required for the building of signal boxes, stations and bridges.

Some older members of family have said that, in their childhood, they were told that their great-grandfather (William), had made bricks for the Chappel Valley viaduct (on the Stour Valley Railway line) and for the Colne Valley railway and Tendring Hundred railway. A 1933 Clacton newspaper containing an obituary of Zachariah, William's fourth son, states quite clearly that William had made bricks for the stations along both lines.

In the early 1870's, William and Emma, together with nine of their twelve children, moved to Clacton to a house in Pallister Road. The 1881 census shows that by then they had moved to No. 6 Brick Kiln cottages, now known as Seabreeze cottages, in Holland Road and only three of their children, William, John Thomas and Agnes were still with them. Zachariah had married Emma Curtis in 1879 and they, together with their year old son, were living next door at No. 5.

Photo: Adrian Corder-Birch collection

COLNE VALLEY VIADUCT, CHAPPEL (c.1900) as viewed from SWAN Street (TEY Road) showing all 32 arches–a view which cannot be seen today.

The 1881 census (Clacton population 651) also recorded that William was a Master Brickmaker employing three men. It is highly probable that by then he had acquired the brickfield at Magdalen Green and an 1882 Directory listed him as owning a lodging house in Rosemary Road.

By 1886 he was in business with his son William trading as William Fairclough and Son, Brickmaker of Magdalen Green. Around that time, he and Emma moved into a house, named 'Southdene', which was quite close to the brickfield.

William and Son had now built up a considerable business supplying bricks to many local builders and were also building houses on their own account.

Suddenly, on 27th November 1889 at the age of 62, the elder William died of a heart attack caused by an epileptic fit. He had suffered from epilepsy for the last two years of his life.

His wife, Emma, died twenty four years later and they are buried together in an unmarked grave in Burrs Road Cemetery. It is a sobering thought that William and Emma who can be said to be responsible for the growth of so much of Clacton have, until now, been just an entry (Plot 108 (B) section H) in the Cemetery Burial Record Book.

Nine of their children settled in Clacton and most played a part in influencing its future development which may become apparent as the reader progresses through the book.

The oldest daughter Emily, married Thomas Cattermole on 11th October 1877 and they had two daughters: Louisa born in 1880 and Margaret born in 1883. At the time of their marriage, Thomas was a stable keeper but later became a general labourer. He was also one of the crew of Clacton's lifeboat the 'Albert Edward' but tragically, together with the second coxswain James Cross, he lost his life when the lifeboat capsized in a gale in 1884.

Very little is known of John Thomas, who is listed in the 1881 Clacton census as a brickmaker, except that he lived with his sister Emily for a number of years before moving to a cottage in Old Road. He kept himself very much to himself.

Also living with Emily was her sister Florence, but no trace has been found of her after 1881.

Stripling, the eldest son, (actually William was the first born in 1851 but he died soon after birth), became a very well known figure in the Hythe area of Colchester after being with his parents in Clacton working as a brickmaker. He had a brickmaking business in Colchester on part of the land now owned by Paxman's. He can just be remembered by a few of the older members of the family as 'Uncle Strip'. His wife's first name was Eliza and they had two daughters, Kate who later married Ted Syrett and Lil who married Jack Baker.

Ada married John Chaplin and had three children, Ada, Emily and Jack. When Jack grew up he married Emily May Bartlett and both were employed by Uncle Zachariah. Emily worked as his housekeeper as well as keeping the books and writing letters and Jack managed his uncle's business whilst he was ill up to his death in 1933.

Agnes married Ernest William Thomas Baxfield, known to his friends as Sam Baxfield and they had two children, Fred and Dorothy. The name Baxfield will be remembered by many for the fishmonger's shop that Sam had at 59 Rosemary Road,

Photo: Kenneth Walker collection

The first Clacton Lifeboat (1878) the ALBERT EDWARD which capsized in 1884.

over a period of many years. Sadly, he died in March 1921, aged 52, but Agnes and the children carried on the fishmonger's business. Sam's father, E. W. W. Baxfield of Yarmouth and Ipswich, was well known at the time throughout the Eastern counties as a fish merchant.

Emma married Ernest Austin and they had four children, Doris, Winnie, Jack and Ernest Percival, the latter of whom later started E. P. Austin, Stonemasons, in Old Road, Clacton, which is still a family run business today.

However, it is William and Zachariah who contributed the most to the growth of Clacton through their many business activities and these will be described at some length. Also the descendants of these two brothers, who total thirty five male members, have ensured that the name of Fairclough is indelibly identified with Clacton.

It was probably not a rash or haphazard decision that William had taken to settle with his large family in Clacton in the early 1870's, but rather that he had appreciated the business opportunities that would arise at this embryo seaside resort.

In 1870, whilst still living in Walton, William had been given the contract to cut the 'Pier Gap' through the cliffs at Clacton to provide easy access to the pier that was being constructed. Doubtless he could then visualise that it was the start of momentous developments and this view was probably reinforced by his talks with Peter Bruff whose ambition and foresight was largely responsible for the birth of Clacton.

Although Clacton had been investigated early in the 19th century as a site for seaside development, nothing could be done in this direction until 1864 as there had been a Trust in the name of Mr. and Mrs. William Watson, which effectively precluded the sale of land or any building work.

However, on William Watson's death, in 1864, the Trust expired and the land, totalling about fifty acres, was put up for sale. This was acquired in 1865 by Peter Bruff a well known Essex civil engineer who had been involved in many East Anglian projects. One such enterprise was the expansion of Walton a few miles up the coast from Clacton. Due to various difficulties, both man-made and natural, Bruff had become disillusioned with the venture and he saw that at Clacton there would be far greater opportunities for making a first class seaside resort. It had very few existing buildings to hamper planned development and it would be possible to expand along the coast and inland.

As the engineer for the Tendring Hundred Railway from Colchester to Walton, Bruff also appreciated that a line could, and should, be built to connect Clacton into the railway network.

He was the instigator of the 'Thorpe and Great Clacton Railway Act, 1866', but that railway never started. Instead, in co-operation with the Woolwich Steam Packet Company, work started in 1870 on building a pier which was completed in July 1871. This could be pinpointed as the birth of Clacton as we know it today and from that time on the Faircloughs began to take their share in shaping its future.

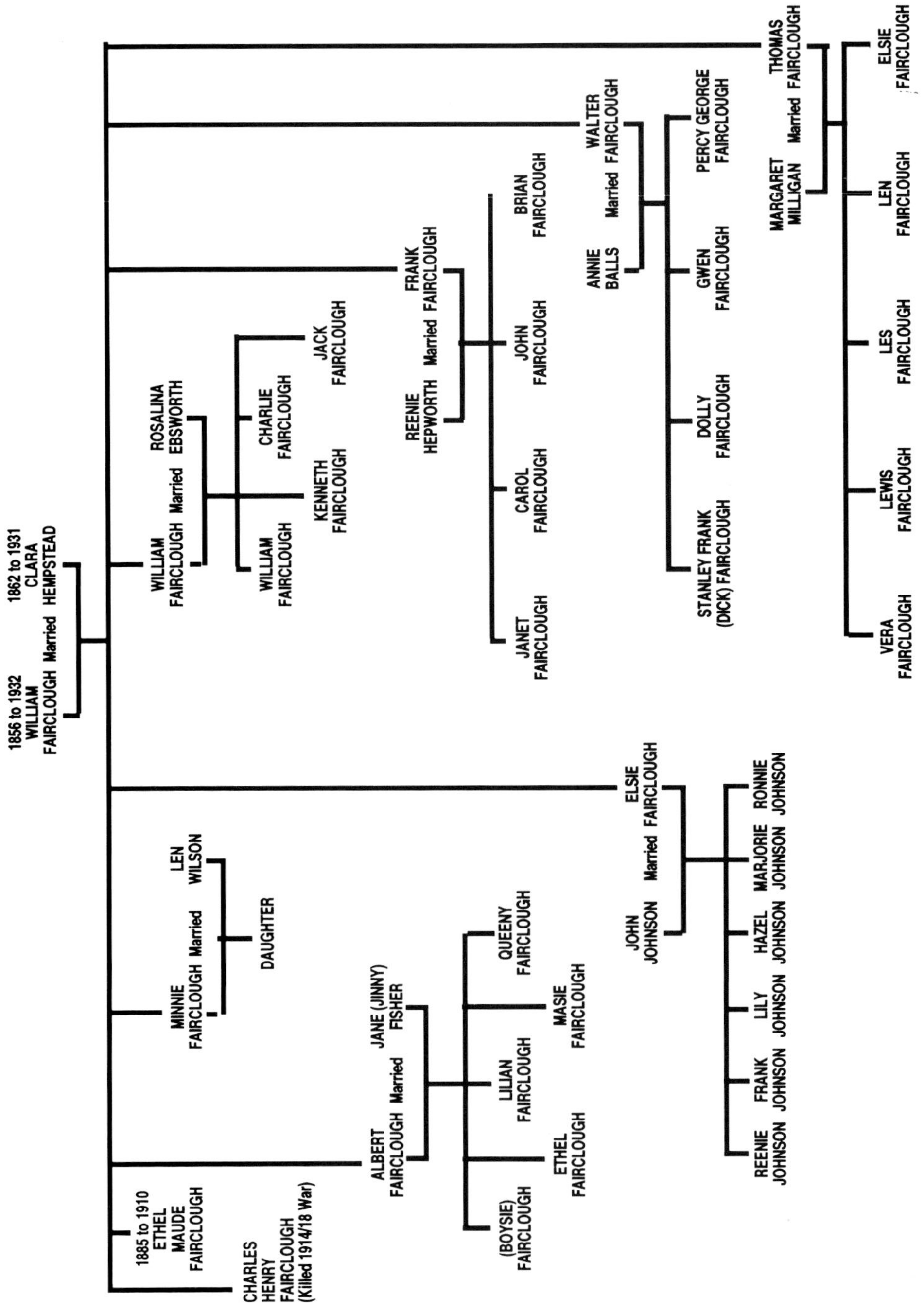
1856 to 1932 WILLIAM FAIRCLOUGH
Married
1862 to 1931 CLARA HEMPSTEAD
CHARLES HENRY FAIRCLOUGH (Killed 1914/18 War)
1885 to 1910 ETHEL MAUDE FAIRCLOUGH
ALBERT FAIRCLOUGH Married JANE (JINNY) FISHER
(BOYSIE) FAIRCLOUGH
ETHEL FAIRCLOUGH
LILIAN FAIRCLOUGH
MASIE FAIRCLOUGH
QUEENY FAIRCLOUGH
MINNIE FAIRCLOUGH Married LEN WILSON
DAUGHTER
ELSIE FAIRCLOUGH Married JOHN JOHNSON
REENIE JOHNSON
FRANK JOHNSON
LILY JOHNSON
HAZEL JOHNSON
MARJORIE JOHNSON
RONNIE JOHNSON
WILLIAM FAIRCLOUGH Married ROSALINA EBSWORTH
WILLIAM FAIRCLOUGH
KENNETH FAIRCLOUGH
CHARLIE FAIRCLOUGH
JACK FAIRCLOUGH
FRANK FAIRCLOUGH Married REENIE HEPWORTH
JANET FAIRCLOUGH
CAROL FAIRCLOUGH
JOHN FAIRCLOUGH
BRIAN FAIRCLOUGH
WALTER FAIRCLOUGH Married ANNIE BALLS
STANLEY FRANK (DICK) FAIRCLOUGH
DOLLY FAIRCLOUGH
GWEN FAIRCLOUGH
PERCY GEORGE FAIRCLOUGH
THOMAS FAIRCLOUGH Married MARGARET MILLIGAN
VERA FAIRCLOUGH
LEWIS FAIRCLOUGH
LES FAIRCLOUGH
LEN FAIRCLOUGH
ELSIE FAIRCLOUGH

William Fairclough (1856 - 1932)

Photo: Fairclough Family collection

WILLIAM and CLARA FAIRCLOUGH

William was born in 1856 at West Bergholt and although the second son of William and Emma, he was perhaps the one most closely associated with his father during the latter's business career. Although his brothers Stripling and John are known to have worked as brickmakers at some stage, William is the only son who was definitely recorded as having worked alongside his father at the brickfield in Magdalen Green. By 1886 they were in partnership trading as William Fairclough and Son, Brickmakers of Magdalen Green and on the death of his father in 1889, William inherited the business.

Meanwhile, early in the 1880's, he had married Clara Hempstead from Brightlingsea and initially lived at Magdalen Green, but by 1892 they had moved into 'Elsie Villa' at 161 Old Road, Clacton, which had been built by William Fairclough and Son together with some of the surrounding houses which today are all shops.

By the turn of the century, William had built up a thriving business of manufacturing bricks and tiles and supplying sand, gravel and loam, as well as house building on a small scale. He had inherited the brickfield at Magdalen Green, now Groom Park, but he also acquired one in St. Osyth Road between Alton Park Road and Coopers Lane where Ford Road is now and another at Coppins Green. The last brickfield that

Photo: Pat Freeman

Part of OLD ROAD, WILLIAM FAIRCLOUGH'S stables were to the rear of the CLACTON AUCTIONS.

he purchased was at Coopers Lane where there was a practically inexhaustible supply of fine brick earth which enabled him to manufacture bricks and tiles in ever increasing quantities to keep pace with the demand as the development of Clacton progressed.

William's business was mainly based in St. Osyth Road, formerly known as 'Guilders' or 'Smith Pit' and it was the main source of supply for most of the materials needed by house builders in the Clacton area. It can be said that there are not many of the older buildings in Clacton that have not got a Fairclough red brick in them.

He had much experience of brick and tile manufacture and was able to produce them with great accuracy and at a price which was cheaper than similar items brought in from brickfields further afield. He also appears to have had first call on the output of several local sand and gravel pits. With a large staff of men and a considerable number of horses and vehicles he was able to supply and deliver orders over a wide area with the least possible delay and this was the key to his success.

William was also in an ideal position to supply to himself most of the materials needed for his own house building business. His efforts in this direction could not compare with those of his brother Zachariah, to whom he also supplied the materials, as he probably only built houses during the winter months when frosts were a hazard to brickmaking.

As mentioned earlier, William Fairclough and Son built 'Elsie Villa', but in 1897 William added a stable and a coach house, with hay loft, to the rear.

Photo: Pat Freeman

Nos. 19 and 21 COOPERS LANE. The bungalow on the left was built by WILLIAM FAIRCLOUGH (1892-1973) and he and ROSALINA lived there.

Photo: Pat Freeman

BLAKEHAM COTTAGES built 1883. To the left of the drainpipe can be seen the ROYAL Insurance fire plaque.

In 1899 he built two semi-detached cottages 'Fairclough Villas' which are numbers 19 and 21 Coopers Lane and in the following year, three houses in Oxford Road, also 12 cottages in St. Osyth Road around 1902, but no others have definitely been recorded.

However, Clacton readers may wish to do a little detective work in this direction as it appears that a Fairclough built house carried a special 'signature'. This can be plainly seen on number 21 Coopers Lane, on 'Blakenham' and 'Harradine' cottages (built 1883) in Old Road and on several houses in Warwick and Key Roads, but there are probably more that carry this 'signature'.

If you look at the picture of number 21 Coopers Lane (on page 31), you will see that the red facing bricks have courses of yellow bricks at various heights as follows: a single course at the top and bottom, two courses above each window the width of the lintel apart and a course level with the bottom of each window. The lintels are also made of the light coloured bricks.

Little is known of William's activities outside of his business dealings, except that he was a founder member of the Clacton Unionist Club and was a staunch conservative.

William and Clara had nine children (see Family Tree page 26), all born in Clacton, but when William died in 1932, soon after Clara passed away in 1931, only six were still alive and they shared the residue of his estate. They were Walter, Albert, William, Thomas, Frank and Elsie (Mrs. J. Johnson).

Photo: Pat Freeman

No. 21 COOPERS LANE showing the 'FAIRCLOUGH SIGNATURE'.

The sons carried on, operating from Coopers Lane, as 'Fairclough Brothers'. Bricks had ceased to be produced at Coopers Lane in the early 1930's and the firm traded as hauliers and suppliers of sand, ballast and gravel. About 1933 Walter's son Stanley Frank, known as Dick, joined the firm and, sadly, in 1934 his father was killed in a motor bike accident outside the Warwick Castle..

Dick was employed to drive a 'new fangled' lorry for his uncle as they all still preferred their horse and carts. Later on, Dick and his wife Maude, took over the running of the business from their home in Carr's Road and continued to do so until 1964 when Thomas died. The brickfield and some of the land had been sold over the previous years, but there was approximately eight acres of land left when William finally decided to wind up the estate. This parcel of land was auctioned by Gardner and Spurgeon at the Station Hotel, Clacton, on 10th June 1964 and it was bought by North East Essex Builders Limited who proceeded to build the estate whose roads have been named after trees.

The Coopers Lane site had been worked for over sixty years and it could be said that it was one of the best purchases the Faircloughs ever made.

Photo: Fairclough Family collection

Believed to be the first committee of the CLACTON UNIONIST CLUB. Back row, 1st left WILLIAM FAIRCLOUGH, 4th left JIM BROOKS, 5th left ERNIE COLE, 6th left FRANK CRISP, 8th left JACK CHAPLIN, 9th left FRANK SURRY. Seated, 1st left BILLY BRETT, 4th left ALF GIBBONS.

Photo: John Hooker collection

The WARWICK CASTLE in Old Road was demolished in 1974.

Zachariah Fairclough (1858 - 1933)

Of all the Faircloughs, Zachariah is probably the one most remembered by older Clactonians.

Photo: Fairclough Family collection

ZACHARIAH FAIRCLOUGH (1858-1933)

Photo: Fairclough Family collection

EMMA FAIRCLOUGH (1857-1915)

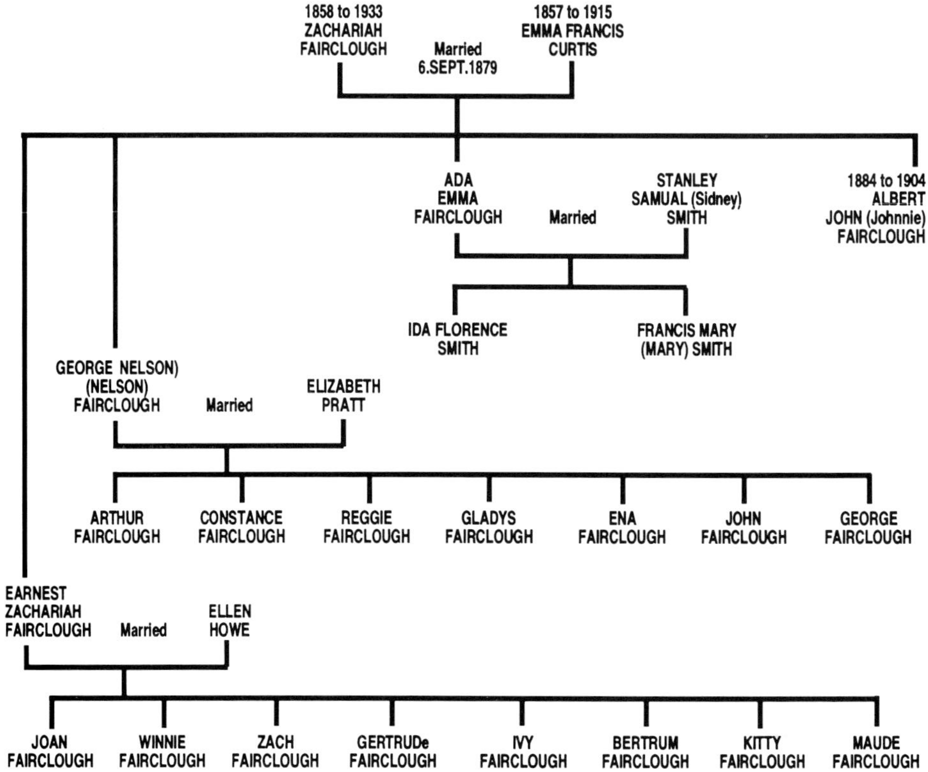

He was the third son of William and Emma and was born at White Colne in 1858. From there on he was constantly on the move as the family went from place to place along the railway lines as they were being constructed, going from White Colne to Earls Colne to Sible Hedingham then to Great Bentley, Kirby, Frinton and Walton, all before he reached the age of fourteen. Consequently, as there was no such thing as the Education Act with compulsory schooling, the sad fact was that he and several of his brothers and sisters received no real basic education.

For a small boy this moving about must have been quite an adventure, but the lack of schooling was, nevertheless, to be a handicap in later life, although Zachariah's inbred grit and determination went a long way towards overcoming it. It also meant that he had to start work at an early age and when only twelve years of age, he was labouring on a local farm at Kirby. Unlike his brothers William, Stripling and John, Zachariah never followed his father into the brickmaking trade. When the family moved to Clacton, by which time he was in his late teens, Zachariah started working for a James Harman as a carter and general labourer.

Photo: Fairclough Family collection

This Tumble Cart owned here by JACK CHAPLIN was almost certainly once the property of his Uncle Zachariah Fairclough. The lad in the cart is Jack's son JOHN and the man is CHARLIE BRUCE who worked for Jack Chaplin.

It was not long before it became evident that he was his father's son insofar as his business instincts were concerned. He began saving hard and when he had sufficient money, he went to the Saturday Colchester Market and bought a horse and second hand cart, thereby gradually building up his own cartage business, which was to be the first stage of his commercial empire.

At the age of 21, Zachariah married Emma Frances Curtis on 6th September 1879. Emma came from a family who lived in the original village of Great Clacton, best remembered as Curtis Brothers, Fish Merchants whose first shop was at 7 North Street, Great Clacton in the 1890's, later having a shop in Station Road, Clacton.

Zachariah and Emma first lived at Brick Kiln Cottage next door to his parents. They had four children, Ernest, George (Nelson), Ada, Albert (Johnnie) and by 1886 they had moved to a cottage in Rosemary Road.

It was around this time that Zachariah's haulage business began to expand and there is evidence that he inherited his father's cartage contracts when he died in 1889. In 1893, to be near the centre of his haulage business, he built a villa, in Jackson Road, which adjoined his garage and stables. He named it 'Fairfield' and he and Emma lived there for the rest of their lives.

Photo: Fairclough Family collection

ZACHARIAH FAIRCLOUGH'S house 'FAIRFIELD' in JACKSON ROAD. Zachariah's daughter ADA can just be seen standing in front of the window. It is believed to have been built by Zachariah in 1893 and it contained four reception rooms and nine bedrooms.

Zachariah's Haulage Business

The growth of a business that started with one horse and cart to that having, at its peak, over 100 horses, could not have been achieved overnight as the logistics of such a build-up must have been quite formidable.

Stables had to be acquired or built, sufficient land for exercising and grazing the horses had to be made available and drivers and grooms had to be hired and trained, besides which there were others in the haulage business against whom Zachariah had to compete for contracts. Nevertheless, no doubt due to a burning ambition and his business acumen, he soon began to win a major proportion of the contracts let by the Clacton Urban District Council, of which there were many of various types. Perhaps the more mundane were for carting stones, presumably needed for road

Photo: Fairclough Family collection

Stables at 'FAIRFIELD' JACKSON ROAD with GEORGE (NELSON) FAIRCLOUGH.

Photo: Kenneth Walker collection

Life boat day at Clacton at the turn of the century. ZACHARIAH had the contract to haul it up and down the beach.

building, and for carting chairs, but Zachariah also carried out street watering, scavenging (refuse collection?), ploughing, grass cutting and hay making. He was also entrusted with the removal of hospital patients and hospital patients with bedding, which seems to suggest that they were expired patients and the latter were from the isolation hospital for infectious diseases and that the bedding would have been taken away for burning.

Zachariah also supplied the horses to pull the first fire engine (the contract calls it 'horsing') in 1895 which he continued to do until 1921 when an internal combustion engine supplanted the old horse drawn 'Steamer'.

As Clacton was being developed the materials needed for constructing buildings, new sea defences and roads were frequently brought, mainly from London, by barges which either tied up at the jetty at the end of Wash Lane or were sailed straight up on to the beach at high tide. In either case Zachariah normally won the contracts, invited by Clacton Urban District council, for their loading/unloading and cartage and he would supply the labour and also the horses and carts for these operations. The work had to fit the time scales of the tides so sometimes it was carried out during the night. It is said that Zachariah's stentorian voice could often be heard emanating from amongst flickering lights as he directed unloading operations–it must have been an eerie scene. Incidentally, he also had a contract for hauling the lifeboat up and down the beach.

Photo: Dick Harman collection

Loading/unloading at LIME KILN WHARF, ST. OSYTH. Centre is an OYSTER SMACK unloading 'five fingers' (starfish) used by farmers as a fertilizer. The barge on the right is the DOVER CASTLE skippered by TAS PAYNE. The barge on the left has been loaded with hay to be taken to London.

Barges on CLACTON'S West Beach. *Photo: Hugh Perks collection*

He was also engaged by local farmers to cart their hay and straw to St. Osyth Creek where his men loaded it onto barges which went to London, returning with manure for use on the farms. These barges were known as 'stackies'.

Records show that Zachariah won all the cartage contracts in connection with the building of the first sea wall in Clacton in 1910. They also gave the costs that he charged for certain types of cartage, typically in 1911, as follows :

2 horses, cart & one man	1/6 per hour	(7½p)
1 horse, cart & one man	10d per hour	(4p)
1 horse, water cart and one man	1/- per hour	(5p)
1 horse, slop cart and one man	10d per hour	(4p)
Unloading barges - flints	1/6 per yard	(7½p)
- brick rubble	1/3 per yard	(6p)

Zachariah was obviously also using many of the horses on his own account in connection with his carriage trade, for his removal business and for transporting materials for his house building operations.

To accommodate all his horses Zachariah had stables in Jackson Road, Warwick and Key Roads and Anchor Road but the majority was kept at Ricebridge Farm (now known as Woodlands Farm) at Little Clacton. Zachariah purchased the approx. 113 acre farm from the Trustees & Executors of GEORGE ALFRED PITCHER who had

Photo: Dick Harman collection

The barge VICTORIA unloading at CLACTON

died on 7th December 1904. The transaction was completed on 28th July 1915 and the purchase price was £1,070. Ostensibly he no doubt purchased this farm as a place to keep most of his horses but it must have been part of his master plan for his future.

As mentioned earlier Zachariah was engaged in the business of house removals using horse drawn pantechnicons. An advertisement of the day shows the vehicle under the heading "Z. Fairclough - Carter & Contractor" stating that furniture could be removed by road or rail and that 'No job was too large or too small" An 'All Risks' breakage insurance was included in the charge.

On December 6th 1933 there was a sale of the late Z. Fairclough's effects as a haulage contractor and included were the following :

one horse, harness, 5 tumbrils, 6 single horse trolleys, timber lorry, pantechnicon, 17 seater 'Bean' motor char-a-banc, 30 cwt. Ford lorry, Standard saloon car, governor's car, contents of blacksmith's shop and sundries.

It obviously marked the end of an era.

Photo: Hugh Perks collection

The barge VICTORIA owned by SNEED DEAN was often to be seen at CLACTON. In February 1900 heavy seas drove her up the beach to within a few yards of the sea wall before she was secured, thus saving her from being smashed up. In the distance is the Tower Hotel and the Grand Hotel.

RICEBRIDGE FARM in its early days. *Photo: Brian Essam collection*

Photo: Brian Essam

RICEBRIDGE FARM now known as WOODLANDS FARM. Although a great deal of alterations and extensions have taken place the original farmhouse is still within the existing walls.

Z. Fairclough

CARTER & CONTRACTOR,

Jackson Road,
Clacton-on-Sea.

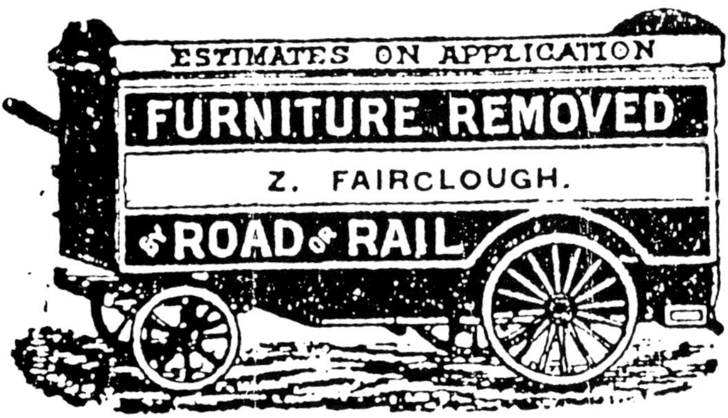

FURNITURE REMOVED

To all Parts in Large Pantechnicons, and Packed by Experienced Men.

No Job too large; none too small

Steam Rollers

"The area was in an uproar. Shopkeepers closed their stores, children ran crying to their mothers, horses bolted and dogs barked themselves into a frenzy. The world's first steam roller had appeared."

Those headlines which appeared in a Kent newspaper in 1865 were inaccurate, in one respect, as the first steam roller had been built by Monsieur Louis Lemoine who demonstrated it in Paris in 1860. Also, the first British built steam roller had appeared in 1863. The roller referred to in the newspaper article was designed and built by the firm who were to become pre-eminent in that field, namely Aveling and Porter of Rochester, Kent.

It is almost certain that the writer of the article could not have guessed at the important part that rollers were to play in the construction and upkeep of our roads. Also Zachariah Fairclough, who was then seven years old, could not have appreciated that he would be heavily involved with them in about forty years time.

It is generally accepted that our first true road makers were the Romans, who invaded Britain during the first century. When they departed from these shores, in AD 411, they left behind them a network of about 10,000 miles of well constructed roads. They had realised that compaction and consolidation of the materials used, especially in the foundations, were essential requisites for the making of good, long lasting roads and for this they employed special ramming tools, called punners, and beaters to obtain the necessary solidity for each layer of material.

Although primitive hand hauled and from 1817 onwards, horse drawn rollers had been used for road making and repairs, it was a happy coincidence that the steam roller was invented just at the time when a great surge forward in road building was required to cope with increased trade and expansion of new towns, or perhaps villages into towns, of which Clacton was a prime example.

The consolidation work on most of the early new roads was almost always entrusted to specialist Steam Roller contractors one of whom, in the Clacton area, was the firm of Donald Mackenzie and Sons. Whilst not in the same league for size as some other East Anglian firms such as Doran Brothers of Thetford, Norfolk, W. G. Smoothy and Sons of Rochford, Essex and The Essex Steam Roller Association of Southend (Offices) and Kelvedon (Works), Donald Mackenzie and Son must have been one of the very first firms in this field.

Established by 1888 as General Merchants, Builders and Contractors, it was, in 1892, advertising a Steam Roller for hire and during the next ten years the firm had five machines, three Aveling and Porters and two Wallis & Steevens. During this time it seems that they were carrying out contracts for the Great Clacton Local Board and the Clacton Urban District Council. However, Donald Mackenzie died in 1901 and minutes of Council Meetings, researched for this book, show that Zachariah Fairclough was on 13th August 1902 paid £3. 13. 6 (£3.67) for rolling and scarifying and in 1905 he was paid £56. 2. 0 (£56.10) for similar work. Until now, it had been generally accepted that Zachariah had started his Roller business in 1909 when records show that he purchased his first roller. It may be that to take over the contracts from Donald Mackenzie and Sons he had actually hired rollers from that firm on the death of the senior partner.

Photo: Essex Record Office

***AVELING & PORTER** Steam Roller owned by the **ESSEX STEAM ROLLING ASSOCIATION**, on contract to the **Essex County Council** seen here at **SWAN ROAD, BEAUMONT**, near **THORPE**, before 1921.*

The first roller that Zachariah bought was an Aveling & Porter 10 ton machine Works No. 2281 (Reg. No. PU1040) which he acquired on the 18th November 1909 from the Works of Aveling & Porter. It had been returned there by the Hastings Urban Sanitary Dept. who had bought it new on the 8th July 1887, in part payment of a new machine.

In 1925 Zachariah traded it in for £175 against a new Garrett roller Works No. 24706 supplied by G. Thurlow & Sons of Stowmarket, Suffolk (see Appendix 1). It is known that it was sold again in December 1925 to H. Noyce of Chandler's Ford and that it was last licensed in 1935. Zachariah's next purchase was a Garrett 10 ton single cylinder roller which he bought directly from the Garrett factory at Leiston in Suffolk, on 10th May 1911. Its Works No. was 29031 (Reg. No. NO3953) and he named it Clacton Belle. In 1927 it was sold to G. Thurlow & Sons in part exchange for a Marshall 8 ton single cylinder piston valve S type roller Works No. 82206 (Reg. No.TW8155) which Thurlow's had bought new in April 1927. Clacton Belle was later with the well known contracting firm of W. J. King of Bishops Lydeard, Somerset. It was returned to Thurlow's and in 1930 it was with William Rawlings of Collingbourne Ducis, Wilts., and by 1955 was owned by James Crockerell of Durrington, Wilts. Sadly this roller and Aveling & Porter 2281 were at some stage, scrapped.

GARRETT STEAM ROLLER No.29031, the CLACTON BELLE, purchased by Zachariah Fairclough in 1911 and used extensively in the construction of many of Clacton's early roads. Zachariah stands to the left of the roller and Jack Faiers

In March 1914, Zachariah purchased a new Ruston, Proctor & Co. Ltd. 10 ton single cylinder slide valve roller, Works No. 43680 (Reg. No. NO3952). By 1935 this engine was in the possession of B. J. Aldridge and Sons of Pulham St. Mary, Norfolk and, in the early 1960's, it was bought by the present owner who lives in the Stamford area.

Zachariah then acquired two more Garrett rollers both 10-ton compound machines. The first he bought new from the Garrett factory in September 1922, Works No. 34165 (Reg. No. PU1042), which he named 'Clacton Queen' and the other Works No. 34706 (Reg. No. PU7494), named 'London Belle', he took in part exchange for his Aveling and Porter, works No. 2281, from G. Thurlow and Sons who had bought it new in March 1925.

RUSTON & PROCTOR steam roller with 'Steam Roller Jack Fairers' at the controls. *Photo: Trevor King collection*

Photo: Pat Freeman

The CLACTON QUEEN at rest on a farm at CASTLE HEDINGHAM.

Both these Garretts and the Marshall were eventually sold to A. M. Emeney of Hadleigh, Suffolk. The Marshall is presently in preservation in the Norwich area but, sadly, the Garretts are very much in need of restoration as they rust away on a farm at Castle Hedingham, Essex, where they have been since 1964.

Originally employed by Zachariah to unload barges at Clacton jetty, a Fred Faiers is known to have driven several of the rollers and indeed, to many older Clactonians, he was affectionately known as 'Steam Roller Jack'. His daughter can remember him rising very early on Monday mornings to cycle all the way into Suffolk from Clacton, when working on contracts for the Suffolk County Council.

Most steam rolling contractors owned at least one living van. This was towed by the roller and when working a good way from base provided an acceptable 'home from home' for the Driver and his Mate as it contained bunk beds, a coal stove, cupboards and cooking utensils. 'Steam Roller Jack' lived in one of these during the week then cycled home to Clacton at the weekend.

Perhaps all this travelling and living away from home for most of the week proved too much for 'Steam Roller Jack' as, in March 1925, he found employment with the Clacton Urban District Council driving their newly acquired roller.

This was a double blow for Zachariah for, as well as losing a most able driver, the Council was now able to do some of the rolling and scarifying on its own account.

Photo: Trevor King collection

The LONDON BELLE with 'Steam Roller Jack' at the controls. This picture shows a typical road making gang.

Photo: Pat Freeman

FOWLER Steam Roller 'BONNIE LASS' owned by TREVOR ELLIS of Chelmsford returning home after a rally in 1990, showing the towed Living Van.

Photo: D. J. Philpott collection

BURRELL Steam Roller No. 3244 when owned by Zachariah Fairclough.

(left)
BURRELL Steam Roller No. 3244 in March 1966 at the KELVEDON depot of the Essex Steam Rolling Association as discovered by MR. CHAPMAN of FILBY, GT. YARMOUTH.

(below)
BURRELL Steam Roller No. 3244 at the 1991 HENHAM Rally.

Photos: Pat Freeman

As early as 1911 they had investigated the pros and cons of having their own roller, but at that time had decided against it.

However, further costings were carried out in 1924 (see Appendix No.2) and these suggested that financial savings would be made if they had their own roller and on 17th March 1925, an Aveling and Porter 10-ton piston valve single (believed to be Works No. 11171 Reg. No. PU6775), was delivered to the Council. This had been selected from quotations by fourteen different firms and the prices ranged from £752.11.0 to £990.0.0. (See Appendix 2). The price for the Aveling and Porter was £813.5.0 less £10.16.0 for a patent sprayer which the Council did not want.

On the same day that the roller was delivered, a committee sat down to consider thirteen applications for the position of Steam Roller Driver and it was finally agreed that the choice would be Jack Faiers of 88 Warwick Road, who would receive £3 per week as wages.

Although Clacton Council had its own roller, Zachariah acquired another one as he now had contracts with other authorities. This machine was a 1910 10-ton single crank compound Burrell Works No. 3244 (Reg. No. TA 2141). This had originally been bought by Fred Payne, of Red Ball, Devon, but when an auction of his assets was held on 6th August 1926 Burrell's, who were owed a lot of money by Fred Payne, acquired the title to the roller (as well as to another Burrell roller Works No.3411). It immediately passed to Thurlow's who straightaway sold it to Zachariah. The date of the transaction is shown in Thurlow's Engine Record Book as 2nd October 1926 but supplementary notes indicate that the roller was delivered to Zachariah directly from Devon very soon after the auction and it would appear that the recorded transaction was held over until the purchase money was paid on the 2nd October 1926. It is remembered as having been fitted with twin scarifiers and that Arthur Burfield was one of its drivers. By 1948 it was with R. F. Fenn, of Frating, and in 1965 it was 'discovered' at the Kelvedon Depot of the Essex Steam Roller Association up to its axles in mud and minus all its brass work. It was then dug out and it spent the next few years at Rowhedge. In 1973 it was moved to Filby, Great Yarmouth, where, in 1988, after 22 years of renovation work, it attended its first rally in all its old glory.

Fire Services

As Clacton expanded it was realised that there was a need for the town to have a Fire Brigade and in June 1893 the Great Clacton Local Board discussed its formation as applications for membership had already been received. Until then the only fire fighting equipment of note available was ladders, which were initially kept at Mr. Cheald's premises, the Castle Restaurant, for which he charged £5 per annum for storing them there in a shelter. Later they were moved to the Board's Yard at Colne Road.

By July 1894 the Board had advertised for a suitable site on which to erect a Fire station and this was found in Skelmersdale Road. It would appear that Donald Mackenzie & Son built a Fire station there and leased it to the Board, initially for seven years. In August 1894 the Fire Brigade was formed with rules and regulations unanimously agreed by the Board and the first eight members were recruited. A horsedrawn fire engine with a steam operated pump was ordered from Merryweather. It was their model 'Metropolitan' capable of raising steam to working pressure within 10 - 12 minutes and the Board asked for it to be named 'Clacton'. It was delivered at Christmas time and in February 1895 it had its first trial with Albert Shulkins, a Board Member, acting as engineer and it was satisfactorily carried out.

Merryweather & Son had charged the Board £2.2.0 (£2.10) for their assistance during this trial. In May 1895 harnesses were purchased at a cost of £13.13.0 (£13.65) and the contract to supply the horses to pull the engine was let to Zachariah Fairclough.

The Clacton Fire Brigade was now in existence and it was not long before it had to spring into action.

On 24th June, at 2.00 p.m. a fire broke out at Clay Hall, Clacton on the property of Phillip Smith. The Fire Brigade was alerted and by the time it arrived it was too late to save the hayrick and straw stack which were totally destroyed. However, the captain of the Fire Brigade Mr. A. R. Robinson and the volunteers were complimented for their efficient turnout and the manner of tackling the blaze. They had arrived at the scene of the fire within half an hour of call out and had raised steam within 12 minutes to pump water from a nearby pond. Perhaps by modern day standards the time scales may seem somewhat long, but it must be remembered that on call out horses had to be obtained and saddled up and taken to the fire station where they were harnessed to the engine and then galloped to the scene of the fire. Also the volunteer crew had little preparation for this first actual operation.

This system of call out was indirectly responsible for one of the great tragedies in the life of Zachariah Fairclough. As mentioned earlier Zachariah had the contract to supply the horses to pull the Clacton Fire Engine and these were available 24 hours a day for that purpose. Initially Zachariah took the horses himself to the Fire station but by 1904 he had handed over the duty to his two sons Nelson and Johnnie (Albert John the youngest son).

The horses were left in Zachariah's stable in Jackson Road and on call out they would be ridden to the Fire station which was by that time in Old Road (on the site of the Waterglade Shopping Centre).

On 12th November 1904 a fire started at the rear of Station Road and the fire bell at 11.10 p.m. alerted Nelson and Johnnie who proceeded to the stable to obtain the two horses. Nelson set off first but soon after he arrived at the Fire Station Johnnie's

Photo: Eddie French collection

CLACTON'S first fire engine outside the Fire Station in Old Road. JOHNNIE FAIRCLOUGH with the reins, taken before November 1904.

Photo: George Hardwick collection

The fire engine seen here in action at a stock fire at CANN HALL FARM in 1906.

horse appeared riderless. It was realised that Johnnie must have met with an accident and a few minutes later Police Sergeant Lancum, on his way to the Fire Station, stumbled across the bleeding and unconscious body of Johnnie. He had, literally, stumbled upon Johnnie because the street lights had gone out at 11.00 p.m. and the road was in complete darkness.

At the inquest, as Johnnie died three days later from acute meningitis as a result of his injuries, it was established that as he was galloping along, about fifty yards from the station, he hit a branch of an overhanging tree. The force of the impact had taken him clean off his horse and he received a fractured skull where he was struck just above the left eye.

It was agreed that the tree was a danger to riders and should be cut down and that all street lights leading to the fire station should be left on all night.

Johnnie's funeral took place on 18th November 1904 and the funeral procession to Great Clacton Cemetery (Burrs Road) was led by the Clacton Fire Brigade headed by Capt. C. F. Hill and Superintendent Wall. Thirteen mourning coaches were behind the hearse followed by all of Zachariah's employees, about forty in all. Johnnie who was Zachariah's favourite son, was only 20 years old and he was joined in the same grave by his father and his mother Emma when they passed away.

Photo: Kenneth Walker collection

Outside the Fire Station in Old Road. Photo taken on August 2nd 1908.

In April 1905, £250 was paid to Johnnie's family by the Clacton Urban District Council as compensation for his untimely death.

Zachariah continued to supply the horses for the fire engine until 1921 when a new motorised engine was bought. It is known that Clacton Urban District Council paid Zachariah £9 on 10th June 1900 for 'horsing a fire engine for 1 year and for 3 fires and 5 practices', and £12.15.0 (£12.75p) in 1905 for this facility. Incidentally, the Council did not cancel Zachariah's 'horsing' contract until several months later when he wrote to inform them that it was still in operation.

On 24th June 1921 there was a large fire at Petley's on the corner of Rosemary Road and Pier Avenue which destroyed the hairdressing salon. Some sources blamed the loss on the delay in catching the horses to pull the engine and suggest that this was the reason for purchasing a new motorised fire engine. However, 'The News' of 1st July said that the Brigade had promptly gone into action but the boiler in the steamer had burst which prevented it from being used. The cause of the explosion was witnessed by the late Denny Wilson, a well known self-employed engineer who was standing near the engine at the time. He told his wife, Ada, that he had seen a brick on top of the safety valve which had been placed there to raise as much steam as possible. Unfortunately the brick was left in position too long and the explosion had occurred. Denny remembered it clearly as a piece of metal had been driven into his cheek. The estimate for the repair of the steamer was £470 and the cost of a new motorised one was £2,141.10.0. (£2,141.50) (Merryweather) or £2,110 (Dennis).

Photo: Eddie French collection

MERRYWEATHER Fire Engine No. NO4104 purchased to replace the horse drawn METROPOLITAN.

Photo: Brian Essam

CLACTON'S present Fire & Rescue Engine with the 'WHITE WATCH' crew. From left to right: JOHN SMITH, STAFFORD (HENRY) FINBOW, RICHARD PLUMMER, Leading Fireman RICHARD NUNN, MICHAEL McCATHIE, STEPHEN (REG) HAWKINS, JIM (HUGHEY) GREEN and PETER (DES) COX.

After due deliberation it was decided that a motorised fire engine should be purchased from Merryweather. Until such time as this could be delivered Merryweather loaned the Fire Brigade another Steamer which saw action in August 1921 when it was used to put out a fire at Gt. Clacton.

The difference of having the horse power under the bonnet instead of between the shafts was very noticeable as the time from 'call out' to that of reaching the scene of the fire was considerably reduced and there was no waiting period to get up steam as pumping could commence almost immediately on arrival.

Surprisingly though, the difference of the volume of water that could be projected onto the seat of a fire was not great. The horse drawn Metropolitan was capable of pumping at just over 260 gallons per minute, whilst the motorised engine could reach 300 gallons per minute. It is interesting to note that Clacton's present day Fire and Rescue vehicle, a Dennis, can pump at the rate of 1000 gallons per minute.

Brake Proprietor and Charabanc Owner

Although, by 1901, the population of Clacton was only seven and a half thousand, during the year there had been over a quarter of a million visitors. This number had gradually built up over the preceding ten years as also did Zachariah's business as a 'Brake Proprietor'.

The terminology 'Brake Proprietor' covered the ownership and use of various horse drawn vehicles such as brakes, wagonettes, landaus, pony phaetons and charabancs. Zachariah, with his 100 or so horses, was well placed for a good share of the business, which was required to cope with not only residents but the great influx of visitors who were keen to see places of interest in Clacton and the surrounding district.

A brake was a general horse drawn utility vehicle derived from the first wagonette. Introduced during the late 1860's, it was drawn by either a pair or four in hand.

A larger version, the Body Brake, had longitudinal seats facing inwards and was used mainly for sightseeing trips and public outings, or it could be used solely for carrying large items of luggage. It could therefore have been used as a station wagon or baggage cart as well as for outings. It was normally pulled by either a pair or a single horse and was entered by means of a rear door and steps as was the wagonette which had been introduced in the early 1840's.

Photo: Fairclough Family collection

TOM FAIRCLOUGH driving, JACK CHAPLIN in carriage. Taken in AGATE Road.

Photo: Fairclough Family collection

GEORGE (NELSON) FAIRCLOUGH at reins. Corner of HAYES Road and ROSEMARY Road.

The landau, originally imported from Germany, was a semi-closed carriage with a double hood so that it could be used in all weathers and was drawn by either two or four horses.

The char-a-banc, a French word for wagon or cart with a seat, was introduced to Clacton in 1900 when Zachariah purchased two of them. Although horse drawn, they were the forerunners of the motorised charabancs which were to come along a little later. They were usually pulled by a four in hand and they had cross seats for seven persons, but could be fitted with extra seats to accommodate school parties, or the like.

It is not known how many carriages of all types Zachariah owned, but as Clacton, by the start of the twentieth century, had a quarter of a million visitors a year, he must have realised the earnings potential of having a good number available.

Others must have thought so too because in 1910 Zachariah, together with Arthur Clark and Ernest Moses Appleby, started the 'Clacton Brake Service' which initially ran scheduled services from a stand in West Avenue. This combined business was operated separately from each of the three's own Brake operations, where Zachariah and Arthur Clark had stables close to each other and Ernest Appleby ran 'The Orwell Brake' from Orwell Road.

Between them the three men held most of the issued brake and carriage licences which, in 1912, totalled 39 Hackney carriages, 1 Omnibus, 2 Bath chairs and a Motor car.

Photo: Fairclough Family collection

ADA and SID SMITH with their 2 year old daughter IDA. ADA was ZACHARIAH FAIRCLOUGH'S daughter. Taken c.1909.

In August 1910, the schedule of prices advertised by 'The Orwell Brake' were as follows:-

Start and Return to West Avenue	Depart	Return	Fare	
St. Osyth Priory	10.30 am	12.30 pm	1/-	(5p)
Harwich/Dovercourt	10.30 am	7.00 pm	3/-	(15p)
Dedham	10.30 am	7.00 pm	3/-	(15p)
Frinton and Walton	2.30 pm	5.15 pm	1/6	(71/2p)
Weeley Woods	2.30 pm	5.30 pm	1/6	(71/2p)

It must have been a splendid sight in those days to see so many horse drawn carriages on the streets of Clacton. Especially so as each one was made of the finest materials available and the finish would have been superb as some 18-20 coats of paint, mainly green and brown, were used to impart a brilliant gloss.

Gradually, however, the internal combustion engine began to make an impact, starting from 1905 when a Mr. C. F. Barnes was issued with a Public Drivers Licence for his charabanc 'Swiftsure' (nicknamed NEVERSURE because of its irregular time

Photo: Fairclough Family collection

Zachariah Fairclough's 'SUNBEAM' showing its iron wheels. Driver HARRY PETCH.

Photo: Mick Baldry

The 'SILVER QUEEN OMNIBUS SERVICE' of the 1920's. Clacton's best remembered charabanc business taken over in 1932 by the Eastern National. 3rd left G. WILSON (known as the timetabler). 5th left Mr. WOOMBALL SENIOR, 6th left Mr. WOOMBALL JUNIOR, 11th left JACK CROSS.

Photo: Fairclough Family collection

Taken on 19th August 1926 going on an outing to BRIGHTLINGSEA Flower Show. CLARA FAIRCLOUGH is the seventh person from the front.

keeping), and in 1913 Mr. P. W. P. Allen registered the 'Silver Queen Omnibus Service' which in 1932 was taken over by the Eastern National. Zachariah may have started in this field around 1920, but the first entry that can be traced, in the Motor Transport Year Book, was for 1924. The charabanc was called 'Sunbeam' and seems to have been a Daimler 28 seater. Many of these charabancs were converted lorries, surplus after the First World War, which were made by such firms as Daimler, Leyland and AEC. Zachariah's 'Sunbeam' and Mr. Barnes' 'Progress' charabancs did 'Mystery Tours' which provided a great attraction for visitors to Clacton.

In 1929 Zachariah bought a new Bean 19 seater, but it is not certain if it was in addition to, or a replacement for, 'Sunbeam'.

Zachariah's charabanc stand was in Meredith Road outside one of his properties where, in November 1926, he was given 21 days notice by the Council to repair damage to the footpath that allegedly had been caused by his charabanc. He was reluctant to do this, but later came to an agreement with the surveyor and reinstated the footpath in January 1927.

Most of these magnificent coaches had their bodywork of wood construction, which was at all times open to the elements. Consequently, over a period, few survived intact, but as the chassis were sound, many were converted back to lorries. This may have been the fate of Zachariah's 19 seater Bean which was one of many items auctioned off on 6th December 1933 by E. J. Gilders and Co.

Builder and Property Owner

Zachariah was a 'Bricks & Mortar' man, not one of the 'Stocks and Shares' Brigade. No doubt this may have been because he could not understand the workings of the Stock Exchange as he could neither read nor write. Nevertheless he was astute enough to build a steady stream of houses from 1893 onwards, most of which he rented out to provide him with a good income and at one time he was the highest ratepayer in Clacton as he owned around 100 houses. He also judiciously purchased land from time to time, some to build on, some to graze his horses on and, if the time and price were right, some to sell.

It is known definitely that he built houses in Warwick, Key, Old, St. Osyth, St. Andrews, Hayes, Oxford and Penfold Roads, as well as shops in Old Road including nos. 113 to 119 where the deeds state that they can sell any goods but bricks, presumably to protect his brother William's brickfield interest.

Zachariah owned a large tract of land adjacent to Rush Green Road where he built three cottage–known as 'Ivy Terrace'. Parcels of land were gradually sold off with one piece going to the Clacton Urban District Council in 1925 on which the refuse tip and Clacton Town Football Ground now stand. Other pieces were sold to Copping Hall Farm (known to many as Brown's Farm) and to Smith's Farm where the Smith family actively farm today.

Photo: Brian Essam

Houses in Warwick Road

Photo: Pat Freeman

No. 27 Key Road. ESTHER FAIRCLOUGH, recently deceased, lived there.

Zachariah also owned land in Alton Park Road between Alton Park School and Ford Road, being parts of Crayers Farm. In 1913 he also acquired a 10 acre site at Botany Lane, Little Clacton, which included three roads that have since disappeared.

Records show that in 1928 he was the owner of Brook Farm which is destined to be the site, in the near future, of a large leisure and shopping complex.

On 28th July 1915 Zachariah purchased, for £1,070, a 113.5 acre farm called Ricebridge which is today known as Woodlands Farm and this was from then on the principal 'home' for his horses. Next to the farm, which is situated opposite the end of Tan Lane in Pig Street, Zachariah built a row of cottages, presumably to house his workers on the farm. During the second world war these cottages had to be painted white so as to give RAF pilots, returning from forays over Europe, a landmark to use in conjunction with the nearby railway line. Today there is, in the field behind the cottages, the Clacton Beacon which is regularly used by aircraft.

From the above brief account it can be seen that Zachariah was a most influential 'Bricks & Mortar' and property man and it was a proud boast of his that he once placed a single order with a Peterborough firm for 3,000,000 bricks which gives some idea of the extent of his building activities (presumably his brother William could not keep pace with his demands).

Photo: Brian Essam

'IVY TERRACE', RUSH GREEN Road (1993).

Photo: Pat Freeman

PIG Street, Little Clacton (1993).

Road Building Contracts

As far back as Roman times it was recognised that the provision of an adequate foundation for a road is essential regardless of the type of surface to be adopted. It will, however, vary depending on the character of the sub soil and the weight and intensity of the traffic to be carried.

Towards the end of the last century when the line of a new road had been established, the top soil was removed and a 3 to 6 inch course of clinker ash would be laid down. This would act as an insulating layer and prevent the capillary creeping action of water and over this hard-core would be spread and rolled to a depth consistent with the weight of traffic being catered for. A layer of smaller stones or flints would then be placed over the hard-core so as to fill the interstices and the whole lot would be re-rolled.

There were then different types of surfacing that could be used and an early one was water bound macadam. For this a film of sharp sand or sweepings was spread over the surface and was then well watered. This was puddled into a slurry as a roller was worked to and fro after which it was left to dry out. It had then formed a surface hard enough to cope with the traffic of the day. A more durable surface was made by brushing and spraying tar onto the road and then spreading chippings over and rolling them in.

Photo: Bernard Bartram

Emulsion being poured onto the old road surface and granite chippings are being spread on top. The roller waits in the background to do its compacting work. Members of the Road Roller Association are carrying out the work as it would have been done years ago.

Photo: Bernard Bartram

The Fowler Steam Roller rests alongside the TAR BOILER, WATER CART and other road building artefacts.

An even longer lasting skin was to make up a mixture of stones and tarmac to make Tarmacadam which was spread over the surface and compacted by a roller. A variant of this was asphalt, a mixture of sand and bitumen, which was spread hot and then rolled, generally with a special quick reverse roller.

Soon after the First World War a very hard wearing surface was obtained as a result of building a road using the 'sandwich system'. For this a layer of stone was spread on a prepared foundation and lightly rolled and over this was spread cement mortar followed by a second layer of stone. This was then rolled to consolidate it and to force the mortar upward between the stones and after the mortar had set it left a relatively smooth but very hard wearing surface.

Whichever method of road making was used, a road roller was an essential tool for compaction. Where existing roads had to be resurfaced, a roller was again essential as its scarifier (see page 73), was used to tear up the old surface.

Zachariah had laid and sewered many of the principal roads in Clacton, as well as some in Colchester, Dovercourt and Harwich and he also had road building contracts with Suffolk authorities.

Photo: Pat Freeman

A close up of a SCARIFIER attached to the rear of a steam roller.

The earliest documented evidence to be found of Zachariah's road building activities in Clacton is that in March 1899 his tender for making High Street (cost £1,259) and Back Station Road (cost £188) was accepted by the Clacton Urban District Council.

Some of the other roads in Clacton known to have been made by Zachariah are Crossfield, Fairfield, Key, Warwick, Alton, Thoroughgood, Walton, Penfold, Herbert, St. Paul's, Victoria, Russell, Priory, Page, Anchor, Hayes, Ellis, Beatrice and Arnold Roads and also Marine Parade East. It says much for Zachariah's business acumen and integrity and the quality of his work that the Clacton Urban District Council entrusted so much of their road building to him. It is perhaps as recognition of this fact that the present Tendring District Council will be naming a new road after the Fairclough family in the near future.

Photo: Brian Essam collection

Many men were engaged by the Council for road building purposes to provide relief for unemployment. This 1922-23 photo shows some working on LONDON Road which was an extension of CENTRAL AVENUE.

Demise of Zachariah Fairclough

After a long and painful illness, Zachariah passed away on 18th September 1933. For several years previously, he had entrusted the running of his business to his nephew Jack Chaplin, son of his sister Ada, as he was not in a position to adequately run it himself. Nevertheless, although suffering greatly, he was still interested in all that went on around him. He welcomed any news of the day from friends or visitors and would reminisce at length about the days when Clacton consisted of a few houses and how he, and his first wife Emma, occupied one of them which was on the site of the Carlton Hotel.

He never tired of talking about the busy life that had been his lot and in May 1933 he told a local newspaper reporter that he worked '9 days a week' when building the sea wall and that nothing could be achieved without hard work. When the article appeared, it concluded with these words "In the evening of his life, old friends wish him peace and consolation that should surely follow a long span of usefulness."

After his death, newspapers described him as a great character and one of Clacton's true pioneers who had been actively associated with the development of the town from its very early days. He had been in business in Clacton for over fifty years and had built up a very successful empire from humble beginnings of buying second hand carts from Colchester Market and in today's terms, would be described as a millionaire business tycoon. He had done all this by hard work and by not being afraid to get

Zachariah Fairclough a few years before he died.

Photo: Fairclough Family collection

his hands dirty. What is truly remarkable was that he had achieved it all without being able to read or write!

To the outside world he may have appeared as a rough and ready character, but underneath he was a very kind man and there were many in his lifetime who had to thank him for acts of kindness toward them, which he never publicised. He was also very sentimental and tears would come to his eyes when he talked about old friends who had passed away. Also indicative of his strength of character was the fact that in those hard drinking days, he publicly declared that he would totally abstain from drink and he kept this pledge for the last forty years of his life.

In Zachariah's will, written on 26th June 1932, he requested that a Trust Fund be formed with Stanley Samuel Smith, his son-in-law, and Joseph William Peacock, his rent collector and accountant, as Executors and Trustees. Later, other Trustees were Henry John Drury and John Archer, who was Stanley Smith's son-in-law.

Zachariah bequeathed his piano to his granddaughter, Ida Florence Smith and another one, by the Imperial Organ and Piano company, to his stepdaughter, Bessie Askew who was also left his gold watch and chain. His daughter, Ada Emma Smith, was to receive rings and his 'Flower Girl' pictures and Emmeline Chaplin (John Chaplin's wife), was left a house named Albert Dene in Oxford Road and also four horses and carts and the use of his yards and sheds in Anchor Road.

His second wife, Bessie, was left a house in St Mary's Road along with a substantial sum of money. Ricebridge Farm, with all livestock and farming implements and the cottages and bungalows, was left to his daughter Ada Emma Smith. His son Nelson was to receive the house No. 12 Warwick Road and his son Ernest, 41 Key Road. The remainder of the estate, including 'Fairfield' in Jackson Road, was to be sold and all the proceeds were then to be put in the hands of the Trustees to supply his three children with an income. Also a Trust Fund was to be arranged for his grandchildren payable to them when they became 21 years of age.

It was at his funeral service at St John's Church, Great Clacton, that the respect and esteem in which Zachariah had been held was testified to by the large attendance outside the Church as well as the packed congregation inside. One of the most touching sights was a band of former employees, with a total of over 150 years service with Zachariah, who were standing outside the church very visibly affected by the occasion.

Included were Mr. W. (Weasel) Wilson, (over 50 years service), Messrs. H. Petch, W. Herbert and A. Gunfield (each 14 years). Mr. E. Gunfield (12 years), Mr. S. Carrington (10 years), Messrs. W. Clarke, F. Jowers and P. Berry (each 4 years), Mr. R. Leggett (3 years), Mr. J. Spooner and F. Taylor (each 2 years) and Mr. R. J. Kittle (20 years). Zachariah had been at one time the largest employer of labour in Clacton and insisted on hiring local men especially when engaged on road contracts.

The Minister of St. John's, the Reverend S. A. Martin, paid great tribute to Zachariah and characterised his life as "a wonderful career". He said that Zachariah "was a man of great decisions and a man of strong personality who had been responsible for important features in the development of Clacton".

There were many tributes to Zachariah from people in all walks of life; general labourers, farm hands, farmers and principal businessmen and traders of Clacton (See Appendix 4 for the list of names).

The second half of the funeral was held in Clacton Cemetery in Burrs Road, where he was buried in the same grave as his first wife Emma, who died in 1915 and his son Johnnie, who was killed in 1904.

Serving Soldiers

Photo: Fairclough Family Collection

Believed to be CHARLES HENRY FAIRCLOUGH.

As with many families, several of the Fairclough line served in the Forces during the Great War and it is known that five close relatives of the brothers William and Zachariah were soldiers although details of their activities are rather sparse.

Three of William's sons served in the army and one was killed by enemy action. This was Charles Henry who was a private in the 9th Essex Regiment after serving as a Trooper in the Essex Yeomanry. He was wounded in France in July 1917 and, sadly, was killed in action on 4th June 1918. This date appears alongside his name on the Imperial War Graves Memorial at Poiziers, France, and in the records of the Essex Regiments. However, on the gravestone of William and Clara, his parents, there is an inscription which reads "...Also in loving memory of our son Charles reported missing in France April 6th 1918". The reason for this discrepancy in the dates is not known.

Charles' brother William was a Lance Corporal in the 1st/5th Essex Regiment and he took part in the landing at the Dardenelles and soon after, on August 14th 1915, was wounded at Gallipoli.

Photo: Fairclough Family collection

WILLIAM (BILL) FAIRCLOUGH (1892-1973)

TOM FAIRCLOUGH (1889-1962)

Photo: Fairclough Family collection

A third brother Tom was at some stage in the Army, but no further details have come to light.

Two of Zachariah's nephews, Jack Chaplin and Ernest Percival Austin, also served in the Army. Ernest was in a machine gun corp, a specialist unit raised from parent regiments. Volunteers for this corps received extra pay and rations as their life expectancy was extremely short. The insignia of crossed machine guns on the left shoulder indicated that the wearer was a marksman.

Photo: Fairclough Family collection

Home from the Dardenelles. WILLIAM FAIRCLOUGH, back row, first left. The huts are probably those of the 2/5th Essex Regiment at Thetford (Norfolk). This was a training and draft finding unit for the 1st/5th Essex Regiment.

Photo: Fairclough Family collection

JACK CHAPLIN
and his wife
EMMELINE

ERNEST PERCIVAL AUSTIN (1890-1947)

Photo: Fairclough Family collection

Many of the Fairclough line served in the second World War and it may be invidious to mention just one–Zachariah Fairclough.

He was a grandson of the Zachariah Fairclough and he also worked for him at one stage. When war broke out, Zack, as he liked to be called, joined the 95th Light A.A. Regiment in Clacton and later on he served as a gunner aboard a merchant ship. In 1942 he was in action on a ship in one of the hazardous Malta convoys and for this he was awarded the Distinguished Service Medal. He survived the war and returned to Clacton where he remained until the late 1950's.

Bits and Pieces

Bits and Pieces, as the name suggests, is a mixture of anecdotes, stories and interesting snippets, some of which have been passed on by members of the family and friends and others that have been extracted from various books and periodicals.

It is hoped that these may help the reader to get the 'feel' of the Fairclough families and the part they have played in the local history of Clacton.

Zachariah Knew How to Strike a Deal

In business there is always someone who has something you want, so when they come to you for something they want that's when the dealing starts.

The Burcart family were, and still are, a very well known Clacton family who in 1927 owned a very nice half-ton Ford van which very much took Zachariah's eye. They also owned land adjacent to his property at 119 Old Road. Ernest Kenneth and Walter Burcart wanted to build a property on it incorporating the wall of 119 and asked Zachariah his price for letting them use it. You can see by the receipt below that it cost them £15 plus the coveted Ford van! If only business was like this today.

RECEIVED of MESSRS ERNEST KENNETH AND WALTER BURCART of Clacton-on-Sea the sum of Fifteen Pounds and a half ton Ford Van (taken in part payment) for the purchase of the right to build into and using the wall on the South West side of their property in Old Road Clacton-on-Sea aforesaid next to my property it being the intention that the said wall shall become a party wall. And to make good any damage. Any further deed required for carrying out this sale to be executed by both parties.

[illegible]

Dated this 13th day of May 1927.

Witness.

A Cold Douche

When Zachariah married the second time, to a widow named Bessie Chittock, it caused a lot of controversy within the family which must have simmered for years before erupting a few days after Zachariah's funeral.

Under the heading 'Executors Unceremonious Reception' the local paper of 7th October 1933 gave a lengthy description of a court case.

Bessie had been summonsed for assault by Zachariah's son-in-law and executor, (Sidney) Samuel Smith, and her solicitor had pleaded guilty on her behalf owing to extenuating circumstances of great provocation.

The gist of the case was that Smith had gone to the house of the deceased to obtain access to various effects but had been confronted, on the premises, by Bessie who told him to clear off or he would have a bucket of dirty water thrown over him. When he refused she carried out her threat not only drenching him but cutting his eye, with the bucket, into the bargain. Smith then roughly pushed Bessie away and for this she cross summonsed him for assault.

After much cross examination the Chairman of the Magistrates bound Bessie over to keep the peace against Smith for 12 months in the sum of £20 and she also had to pay costs of £2.4s. 0d. (£2.20) and her case against Smith was dismissed.

For the record it would have been nice to have discovered the reasons for the animosity of the family towards Bessie but the mist of time has drawn a veil over that particular period.

One for the Guinness Book of Records

In 1820 Thomas Fairclough married Charlotte Howe and in 1826 his brother Daniel married Charlotte's sister Sarah. Much later Jack Fairclough married Kathleen Peck and his brother Charles married Florence (Pat) Peck, Kathleen's sister. After an interval of about 30 years Margaret Fairclough wed Paul Bollu and her sister Susan married Frank Bollu.

Three times two brothers married two sisters in the family tree. This must be a record

Zachariah's Building Lore

Dig the footings of a house on Monday and it would be ready to be moved into on the following Saturday.

.....

He told his bricklayers to lay bricks with a shovel not with a trowel.

.....

There was a saying that if you were getting married you should order your house when the banns were being read and it would be ready on your wedding day.

.....

Photo taken in the 1920's showing from left to right ADA EMMA SMITH (Zachariah's daughter), FRANCIS (MARY) WRIGHT (Ada's daughter), AGNES BAXFIELD (Zachariah's sister), STANLEY SAMUEL SMITH (Ada's husband), ERNEST WILLIAM THOMAS BAXFIELD, known as SAM BAXFIELD (Agnes' husband).

If you did not pay your rent on time, out you would go the next week.

. . . . .

It was said that when the houses in Warwick and Key Roads were being built the scaffolding was left in place until the wallpaper was hung in case the walls fell down. The reason was supposedly that they had been built using sand from the beach but they are still standing, good and strong, today.

. . . . .

It seems that Zachariah never paid his brother William for the bricks and other materials that he supplied to him but instead periodically gave him a house in lieu.

. . . . .

Frank Fairclough, who is the only one of William and Clara's children still alive today, can remember an occasion when he delivered bricks to one of Zachariah's sites. When he asked his Uncle, who was at the top of the scaffolding at the time, where he would like the bricks, the reply he received was "I want them up here boy". So Frank had to unload them from his tumble cart and take them to where he was told

. . . . . .

There was a large tree on the site where Zachariah was to build a cottage in Pig Street. This was cut down but to remove the stump would have been a long job so the cottage was built over it. It is not known which cottage has its own special roots.

A story recounted by several people gives a clear indication of Zachariah's character. He was building one of the shops in Old Road and a telegraph pole was in the way. He asked the authorities to move it but as it was not done on time he just built around it.

.....

Zachariah found another use for his Pantechnicon removal van. He took away one side of it so that on certain jobs his builders could use the Pantechnicon base as a working platform thereby eliminating the need for scaffolding. A farmer from Clay Lane, St. Osyth bought this Pantechnicon at an auction of Zachariah's property and he used it to store animal feed until the late 1970's when it became so rotten it had to be broken up.

.....

Zachariah had a grandson who took his name and at one stage worked for him. Zack, as he liked to be known, was a hard worker but he had one fault–he found it difficult to get up early in the morning. Although he was a hard worker and always made up for a late start, it was not to his grandfather's liking and he was eventually sacked. Obviously Zachariah was not a great believer in nepotism!

Why William?

The first name of William has been popular for many hundreds of years and can be said to be the Fairclough's family name. William has been carried down through the generations from when it was traced in 1793 to almost the present day. It has also caused much confusion during the research into this book the fact being that you hardly know which William you are reading about, i.e. father, son, brother or cousin!

In 1851 William and Emma had a son named William but sadly he died as a very small child. However in 1856 they had another son whom they also named William. Today this may be considered a little morbid by taking away the identity of the first son. You can see here the importance of the name carrying on.

A strange occurrence happened with the William born in 1856 for he had two sons; one born in 1884 and the other in 1891 who were both named William and both were alive at the same time. The first born has disappeared with no further reference to be found of him. The second William (1891 - 1973) also had a son named William, but again, he had died as a child. He had three more sons but none of those was named William. It was here that the family Christian name died as to date there are no further William Fairclough's.

Photo: Fairclough Family collection

ROSALINA FAIRCLOUGH (Julie ESSAM's grandmother) with WILLIAM FAIRCLOUGH (last of the William Fairclough's).

Chappel Viaduct

This magnificent viaduct, now a listed building, was built to carry the Stour Valley Railway over the River Colne. It is over 1,000 ft. long and consists of 32 arches, each having a span of 30 ft. It is said that each arch is 31/2 inches higher than the one preceding it to compensate for the fact that one end of the viaduct is 9 ft. 6 inches higher than the other. Approximately 7,000,000 bricks were used in its construction mainly obtained from a brickfield at Mount Bures (using clamp burning) and at White Colne, where, in all probability, William Fairclough was employed. The viaduct was designed by Peter Bruff and work on it started in July 1847 and it was ready to carry traffic early in 1849. The Marks Tey to Sudbury line was officially opened on July 2nd 1849.

Photo: Pat Freeman

CHAPPEL VIADUCT 1993.

CHAPPEL VIADUCT looking through the middle. See previous picture showing these openings in the supports.

Photo: Pat Freeman

A Plane Tale

A man named Jones once flew a bi-plane, from an airstrip in Alton Park Road, very low along the length of Anchor Road. The noise spooked one of Zachariah's horses which, complete with cart, galloped full tilt down the road and ended up crashing through the plate glass window of a small dairy shop at the end of the road. Result— a little girl was injured and the horse had to be destroyed.

Photo: Brian Essam collec

Press picture of 'THE GENERAL' tragedy.

A Tragedy

In 1937 William (Bill) and Rose Fairclough were living at 'Elsie Villa', 161 Old Road with their three sons, Charles, Jack and Kenneth. Also living there was Rose's father, Albert Henry Ebsworth, whom the boys nicknamed 'The General'. However he did not live in the house with the rest of the family but in a converted shed at the rear.

On Friday 19th November 1937 tragedy struck. A fire, believed to have been caused by an overturned paraffin heater, broke out in the shed whilst 'The General' was in it and despite valiant efforts by Kenneth and Charles, he perished. The two brothers were commended for their rescue attempt at the subsequent inquest.

Keeping on the Right Side of the Track

When Zachariah had his first motor vehicle it was rumoured that he instructed the driver to steer it down single track roads with the nearside wheels on the grass verge and when returning to place the offside wheels on the grass. This was to save wear and tear on the tyres.

. . . . .

Another tale concerning a car is that when he married his second wife Bessie she did not like his new car and refused to go in it. His step-daughter liked it and wished to drive it but Zachariah said 'No'. There must have been many arguments over this car because, by all accounts, Zachariah finally said "If Bessie won't go in it nobody will". He then put it in his garage in Jackson Road and bricked up the entrance. It is believed that the 'car coffin' remained there until his death when the car was exhumed and put up for auction.

Frank Tales

Frank Fairclough used to own a dog called 'Flossie' who always ran alongside his tumble cart as he drove along. However one day a cyclist ran into her and from that day on she ran underneath the cart. Who said you cannot teach an old dog new tricks!

. . . . .

It is said that in his youth Frank took a fancy to a certain Miss Dale, one of two ladies who had a shop on the corner of Carrs Road. However his habit of chewing tobacco, as many did who worked at Coopers Lane Brickfield, was not too well received by the ladies so before visiting the shop he would spit out his plug of baccy into his cap and when he came out he would retrieve it and carry on chewing.

. . . . .

Frank was also fond of a drink and one day he left the pub after having 'one over the eight' and got behind the reins of his tumble cart and headed for home. He was quite proud of the fact that he got as far as Colchester before he was found and brought back to Clacton. It is believed that he was also the last person in Clacton to be prosecuted for being drunk in charge of a horse and cart.

Photo: Fairclough Family collection

WILLIAM and CLARA FAIRCLOUGH with their son FRANK and his dog FLOSSIE.

Guinness is Good for You

At least it was for Agnes, sister of Zachariah, who drank a Guinness every morning at 11.00 a.m. and this saw her hale and hearty into her 90's. Her husband, Sam Baxfield, had a hobby of hare coursing and could often be seen on the Holland Marshes with his greyhounds.

Ghostly Happenings

Gravel pits were once a common sight in Clacton but gradually, as they were worked out, many were used as refuse dumps and when full were sealed and in most cases have been built over.

One or two are now lakes such as that just off Coopers Lane where legend has it that a horse and carriage drove into it and disappeared one dark night and there were no survivors. However, if you are in the right place at the right time and in the right of frame of mind, you may see the ghostly apparition of a coach and horses being driven over the water!

• • • • •

Photo: Pat Freeman

Photo of the lake just off Coopers Lane (1993)

One of William Fairclough's spent pits would have a similar tale to tell, that is if pits could talk, but let the story be told by the local writer and researcher of the supernatural, Wesley H. Downes who, in his forthcoming book, tells it as follows:-

The Ghosts of the German Airmen

A strange story was related by a man who, to this day, clearly recalls an experience that he and two other boys had when he was eight years of age (1953).

Living in Upper Park Road, Clacton, he, together with his two friends, used to play in the nearby disused sand pit and spinney situated off Alton Park Road and St. Osyth Road.

A path leading to the pit was known as Pig Alley, taking its name from the long established piggery on the corner of Alton Park Road.

The boys had been playing in the spinney most of the morning, but tiring of those games, decided to have a look at the three ponds that now formed the remains of the old pit.

As they crossed Pig Alley, they were suddenly aware of three figures dressed in grey uniforms standing by the edge of the largest pond. One was tall with blond hair and seemed to have an injury to one side of his face, he was wearing a flying jacket. The other two were much shorter; all three appeared to have very pale faces.

For some time the boys stood rooted to the spot, until the tall figure held out his hand, palm uppermost. At this gesture the boys turned as one and ran away as fast as their legs would carry them.

The man said that it was not until some time later that he found out that the uniforms which at least two of the figures were wearing were those of the Luftwaffe. (German Air Force).

What the boys did not know was that during the 1939/45 war, on 18th August 1941, a German Messerschmitt 110 fighter bomber was shot down by a Royal Air Force fighter and crashed into the same disused sand pit. Neither the bodies of the crew nor the wreckage of the plane were ever recovered from the mud and water of the pit.

Since that time, the pits have been drained, but there was no sign of the aircraft and the authorities decided to fill the pits with rubbish and eventually build factories on the site, as has now been done.

The actual site where the plane disappeared is concreted over and used as a car park for one of the factories.

There is a strange sequel to this story that some may find hard to accept, but knowing that some very strange things are discovered when investigating the supernatural, one can only try to keep an open mind on the matter.

We have told of the boys seeing three figures, this in itself is rather strange, because the crew of a Messerschmitt 110 was only two, the Pilot and a radio operator/ airgunner, sitting back to back.

Research has revealed that this was indeed so in this case. A man who saw the stricken plane just seconds before it spiralled into the pit, related that he saw the pilot quickly looking from side to side and the airgunner facing to the rear; this was confirmed some years later by the German Air Force records which also gave the names and rank of the crew.

When the plane crashed, the first people on the scene were a man and a teenage youth whose Christian name was Heinz; there was nothing they could do, the plane was completely submerged below the water and mud was splattered everywhere, but strangely, an airman's flying helmet was later found hanging in the branches of a nearby tree and an earpiece from it was found on the ground. A young boy also found a German flying jacket, covered with blood and mud, which he took home but because of the smell coming from it, his father threw it away, but not before he cut off the insignias and emblems from the shoulders.

But the mystery still remains–who was the third figure? Well, this is where the supernatural part comes in. Heinz was duly called up and joined the Royal Air Force as a member of an aircrew.

He had taken part in many operational raids over Germany before he was tragically killed–could the third figure possibly have been his, in some strange way somehow sharing an affinity with the German airmen?

That particular pit has been filled in and built over and strangely enough in the offices standing on top of it today any slight happening out of the normal is always blamed on 'The Germans'!.

Photo: Fairclough Family collection

ZACK, grandson of Zachariah Fairclough.

Dab Hand at Darts

It is not often that someone is remembered mainly for the speed and accuracy with which he could throw darts. Zack, grandson of Zachariah, was such a person and it is strange that his prowess on the dartboard should take priority over the fact that he had won the DSM and was also a member of the Clacton Lifeboat crew. Zack was born in Clacton on June 18th 1911, being the son of Ernest and Ellen Fairclough. Around 1934 he married Rose Moon whose father came from Scotland and her mother Edith Goldsmith came from one of Clacton's old established families. Zack was a builder by trade and is remembered as having helped construct 'Steel Stella' on the Pier at Clacton. 'Steel Stella' was a large Roller coaster and was built in 1937 but was destroyed by fire in 1973. In the late 1950's, Zack left Clacton on his own and headed for the Bahamas where he helped to build a holiday camp for Billy Butlin and later he moved to India where he became involved in the construction of a hospital. Eventually he settled in The Bay of Plenty in New Zealand where he lived for twenty five years before passing away in August 1983.

Zack and Rose had two daughters, Evelyn Rose, now living in Brandon, Suffolk and Ann Maureen living in Bury St. Edmunds. Rose, an active octogenarian, still lives in Clacton.

Loss of the Barge 'Hannah'

On the 3rd November 1886 'Hannah' was off Clacton beach, with another barge, awaiting her turn to unload a cargo of stone which she had brought up from Maidstone. The previous calm weather was replaced by a freshening wind which gradually increased in violence, so much so that both boats decided to run for the shelter of the Colne Estuary. The companion barge made it to safety but, after passing Battery Point, 'Hannah' started to fill with water. The master, Captain Webb, and the crew took to their small boat and soon after 'Hannah' capsized and sank some way off the beach at Priory Spit. A report in the Clacton Graphic said that her cargo of Kentish ragstone was intended to finish off one of the roads in Clacton and that the contractor was disappointed at the loss. Could it have been Zachariah?

• • • • •

Incidentally there was a plan in the early 1880's to build a dock between Wash Lane and the Coastguard Station. A supporter of the plan was Edwin J. Gilder who owned adjacent land. He was an Auctioneer and Estate Agent and the name of Gilder is closely associated with Clacton today. An application was made in September 1894 to the Board of Trade to build the dock at an estimated £2,750. Little interest was shown in the project and only the jetty at the end of Wash Lane was built.

Give–but no Take

A certain Mr. Carrington, had land adjacent to that of William Fairclough's at Coopers Lane and one day William gave him a cart load of horse manure for his allotment which was gratefully received. Expecting a little in return William asked if he could have a few of his cabbage plants and was somewhat surprised to be told "Certainly but they will cost you 2d. (about 1p) each." "But I have just given you a load of manure," replied William, whence came the reply "Well, if you choose to give things away that's up to you, but I don't!"

Miscellaneous Photographs

Photo: Fairclough Family collection

ZACHARIAH FAIRCLOUGH
and granddaughter
IDA SMITH (1910).

Photo: Fairclough Family collection

CLARA FAIRCLOUGH and ELSIE HAYWOOD (Tom's daughter).

Photo: Brian Essam collection

Believed to have been taken at the Conservative Club, Old Road. Standing left to right–Len Randall, Jack Snart, Tiny Revett, Harry Dusty Miller, George Fairclough, Unknown, Olly North, Harry Dowsett, Unknown, Tom Fairclough, Sid Gardner, Jim Webster. Sitting back row–left Ernie Cole and right Jack Chaplin. Sitting front row left to right–Frank Fairclough, Charlie Wilson, Mr. Smith, Andy Wilson, Ralph Watcham and Sid Baines.

Photo: Brian Essam collection

Clacton & District Cycle Club (1927-1936) outside the FLAG INN at FLAG HILL. 5th left JOHNNIE MOORE (Zachariah's blacksmith), 6th left WILLIAM FAIRCLOUGH, 8th left JACK CHAPLIN.

Photo: Fairclough Family collection

Wedding picture of MINNIE FAIRCLOUGH to LEN WILSON. To the immediate right of MINNIE is her twin brother FRANK next to him is JINNY FAIRCLOUGH and then the father of the bride, WILLIAM FAIRCLOUGH. 1st left, back row is Mr. WILSON (the bridegroom's father), 2nd left LOUISE DAY (STRIPLING FAIRCLOUGH'S granddaughter), then Mrs. Mills (Dolly MILLS' mother-in-law). Front row, from the left ROLAND MILLS, Harold MILLS, MRS. WILSON (mother of the bridegroom), LILIAN FAIRCLOUGH, DOLLY MILLS, CLARA FAIRCLOUGH (the bride's mother) and ELSIE FAIRCLOUGH, MINNIE died in childbirth about a year later.

Appendix 1. ***GEORGE THURLOW & SONS***

George Thurlow was born in 1837 at Leiston, Suffolk, and moved to Stowmarket early in the 1870's. By 1875 he had started a business of oil blending, the manufacture of belting and the build, supply and repair of agricultural implements.

He had three sons, two of whom, John and George Reeder, were active in the business. George Reeder, the youngest of the two, was a keen sportsman and was well known for his delight in riding a penny-farthing cycle in all parts of the country (he would take it on a train to the area where he wished to do his riding). When George Thurlow died in 1890 John took over as Manager but his health began to fail and he died in 1906. Prior to that, in 1903, George Thurlow & Sons was formed with George Reeder as Managing Director. In 1914 they took over Woods of Stowmarket which had a foundry in the town.

From early in the century the firm had been Agents for various manufacturers of steam engines, steam rollers, threshing drums and other agricultural implements and from 1903 to 1935 their records show that they sold 368 new traction engines and steam rollers and 865 threshing drums to all parts of the country. They had a thriving steam engine repair business and could make new boilers and fire boxes and, in fact, they had the capability to carry out complete refurbishing.

In 1970 they merged with Frank J. Nunn of Elmswell and in 1985 they did the same with F. A. Standen so that they are now trading as Thurlow Nunn Standen from their Head Office in Elmswell, in Suffolk, with centres at Downham Market, Ely, Kennet, March and St. Ives, which makes them a formidable force in the field of a whole range of sophisticated agricultural machinery.

John, the great-grandson of George (Senior), is the Chairman of the Board of Directors of the company.

Taken at the Suffolk Show 1910 held on the recreation ground in Stowmarket. John Thurlow is 2nd from left and George Reeder Thurlow is 3rd from left. *Photo: George Thurlow*

Appendix 2

RELATIVE COST OF HIRING OR BUYING A STEAM ROLLER

In 1911 an investigation took place by the Clacton Urban District Council to see if it would be more economical to buy its own steam roller rather than hiring it and the decision was to continue to hire.

In 1924, the Clacton Urban District Council surveyor was asked to carry out another review and he produced the following salient facts.

The annual cost of hiring a steam roller from Zachariah Fairclough, including the provision of fuel and use of the scarifier (a device on the rear of the roller for breaking up road surfaces, see Page 73), was approximately £450.

It was stated that the Council could purchase a roller, and build a shed to house it, for £1,000 and this could be funded by a 10 year loan costing £129 per annum. This cost when added to the drivers wages, together with an allowance for fuel, oil and repairs, would total £300, which gave a saving of £150 per annum rising to £279 after 10 years when the loan was repaid.

It was decided to go ahead and purchase a roller and quotations for it were received as follows:

	£. s. d.	
Ruston & Hornsby, Lincoln	820. 8. 0.	(£820.40)
T. C. Aveling & Company, Birmingham	990. 0. 0	
W. Tasker & Sons, Andover	772. 8. 6	(£772.42)
Marshall & Son, Gainsborough	774. 13. 6	(£774.67)
Wallis & Steevens,Basingstoke	872. 10. 6	(£872.52)
Aveling & Porter, Rochester	813. 5. 0	(£813.25)
Robey & Company, Lincoln	756. 0. 0	
Burrell & Sons, Thetford	752. 11. 0	(£752.55)
Armstrong Whitworth, London	821. 10. 0	(£821.50)
Fowler & Company, Leeds	801. 17. 0	(£801.85)
Babcock & Wilcox, London	791. 1. 0	(£791.05)
Clayton & Shuttleworth, Lincoln	758. 16. 0	(£758.80)
T. Green & Sons, London	792. 10. 0	(£792.50)
Barford & Perkins, Peterborough	814. 0. 0	
Barford & Perkins, Peterborough	877. 0. 0.	

The roller chosen was the Aveling & Porter.

The roller was delivered on 17th March 1925, but in January 1927 it required boiler repairs costing £7. This sparked off a controversy as to the amount of money the Council was spending on the roller which led to the Clacton Urban District Council asking its accountant to give the costs, which he gave as follows:

Steam Roller & Scarifier for year ending 31.3.1926

Wages	£126
Insurance	£8
Fuel	£83
Repairs	£30
Tools, etc	£2
Water	£19
Loan charges for the year	£108
1/10th the cost of the shed (£220)	£22
Sub Total	£398
Less hire to private customer	£17
Total	**£381**

Cost of hiring steam roller and scarifier from Zachariah Fairclough:

1923	**£209**
1924	**£231**
1925	**£450**

Further comparative costs:
Council's Steam Roller year ending 31.3.26:

Steam Rolling and Scarifying, with fuel and water	**32/5**	**(£1.62) per day**
Steam Rolling and Scarifying, without fuel and water	**27/-**	**(£1.35) per day**

Zachariah Fairclough's charge for steam rolling, without fuel and water:

1923	**32/-**	**(£1.60) per day**
1924	**32/-**	**(£1.60) per day**
1925	**30/-**	**(£1.50) per day**

An additional charge of 10 shillings (50p) per day was made for scarifying.

Appendix 3

THORPE BRICKFIELD

Whilst researching for this book, the site and remains of a previously unrecorded brickworks were discovered adjacent to Thorpe railway station on the piece of land within the area bounded by the railway line, Holland Brook and Harwich Road.

From the deeds, kindly loaned by Mr. Meek of Holland on Sea, some of its history has been gleaned as follows.

On 30th December 1893 Mr. George Marshall purchased from Mrs. Helen Lowe (whose father had just died), part of a field adjacent to Thorpe railway station. The other part was sold to Mr. W. C. Dancey on 22nd February 1894. George Marshall was a mineral water dealer and he probably acquired the property because there was a natural spring in the field. As bottles have been found on the site, it is assumed that he did carry out bottling water there, but on 17th October 1896 he sold the field to Donald Mackenzie for £420. He was a builder who was erecting cottages close by and probably due to this trade he started a brickworks on the site. The extent of its use is not known, but it is indicative of its production capabilities that a private siding was laid to it from the close by railway line.

Donald Mackenzie died in 1901 and the brickworks, including the kiln and drying sheds, was put up for auction at the Colchester Corn Exchange on 12th September 1903. Walter Hercules Short, a chartered accountant of Colchester, acquired the brickworks on 21st December 1903, but from then on no further details about it are known.

Some remains of the kiln are still standing and it would appear that it had been an 'updraught' type, of rectangular shape. Parts of three sides can be seen and measurements taken indicate that it was 5.25 metres wide and 4.75 metres deep with walls 0.75 metres thick. The route of the private siding is clearly visible although Mr. Meek has said that the rails were removed and sold for scrap sometime in the early 50's. He also said that the sleepers were used to build a bridge over Picker's Ditch at the point where it runs through Valley Farm Caravan Park at Clacton.

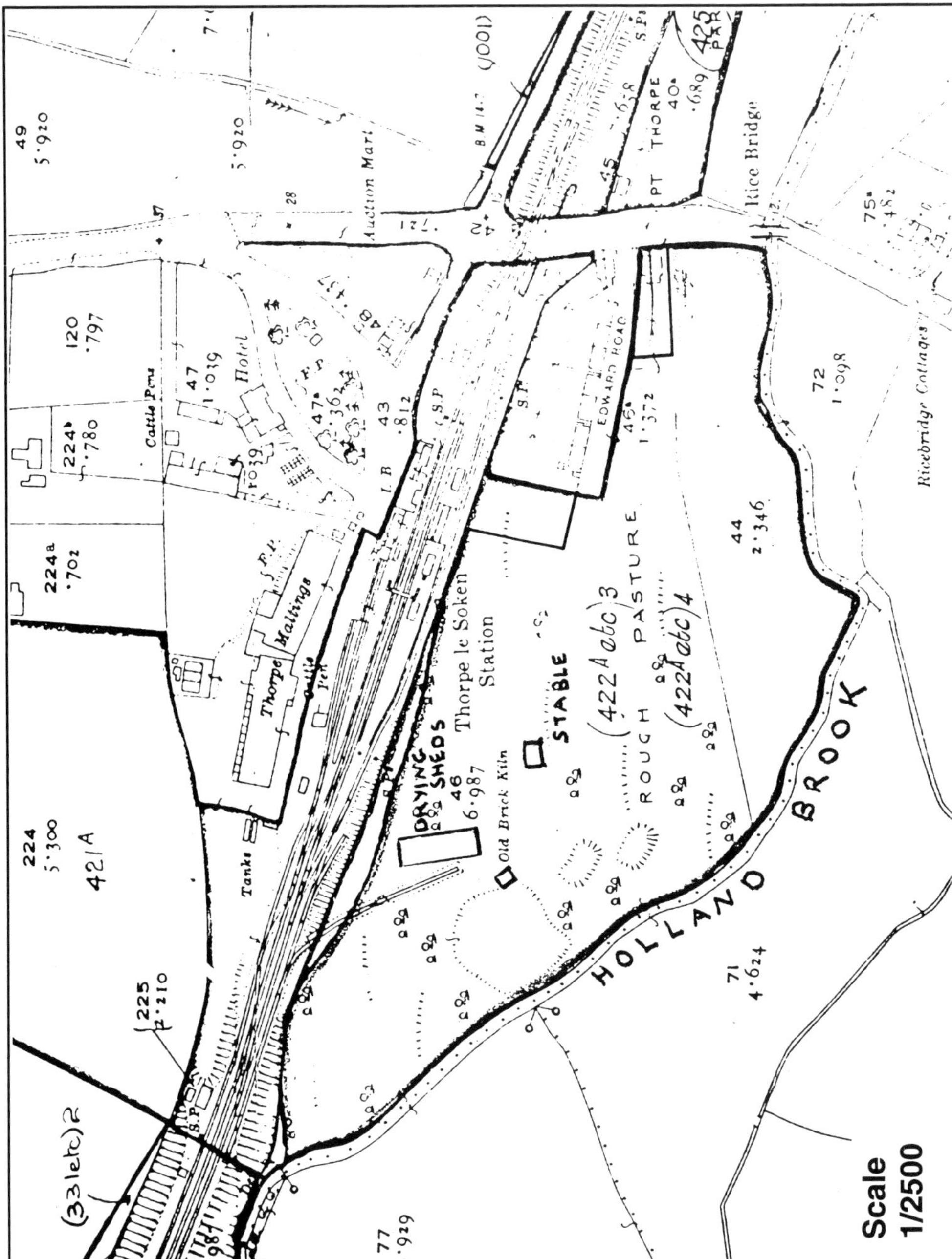

Site of Thorpe Brickfield

Photo: Ken Austin

WALTON BRANCH train at THORPE LE SOKEN station. The driver is believed to be PAUL AMOS and it was his last trip. Just beyond the top end of the platform is where the siding branched off for the Thorpe brickfield. Photo taken around 1960.

Photo: Pat Freeman

West side of the kiln at Thorpe. Brian Essam holding spade (1993).

Photo: Pat Freeman

Brick found on site of Thorpe Kiln. Exact cause of marks unknown.

Photo: Pat Freeman

Thorpe Brickfield showing close-up of north side

Appendix 4

ZACHARIAH'S FUNERAL

As well as members of the family, the following are listed as having attended the funeral.

Superintendent W H Hubbard (Clacton Police)

Mr. E. V. Mann (representing G. T. Mann)

Mr. Wilson Blythe (St Osyth)

Mr. R. A. Fenn (Messrs Fenn Wright & Co)

Mr. W. J. Clarke Cann Hall Farm, Great Clacton)

Messrs F. H. and W. G. French

Mr. H. Lonsdale (Thorpe) and Mr. E. W. Carter

Mr. A. W. J. Ray (Essex & Suffolk Equitable Insurance Society)

Mr. E. W. Crisp (formerly of Clacton Railway station, L.N.E.R.)

Mr. J. Fairwether (former Foreman of Clacton Railway Station)

Mr. E. Leaning (Leaning & Carr Solicitors)

Messrs A. & J. Stern

Mr. S. Weeley

Mr. Partridge

Mr. E. M. Appleby

Mr. S. Chilvers

Mr. S. A. Fitch

Mr. A. W. Kerry

Mr. A. Rampling

Mr. G. H. Smith (Sanitary Inspector)

Mr. E. Newson

Mr. T. Parmenter

Mr. Wagstaff

Mr. F. G. Roberts & Mr. R. Canler (with two employees of Canler & Sons representing the staff of 150)

Captain Hall (Clacton Fire Brigade)

Mr. Miller (representing Messrs A. S. Bullock Limited)

Mr. R. Cane (representing the Clacton News)

Mr. P. S. Howard

Mr. and Mrs. W. B. Carter

Mr. G. H. B. Gould

Mr. E. P. Austin

Mr. A. E. Bignell

Mr. W. Tomlin (E. J. Gilders and Co.)

Mr. and Mrs. A. Bareham

Mrs. E. Kingsman

Mr. J. Moore

Mr. J. W. Peacock

Mr. and Mrs. S. Chittock

Mr. L. C. Bryan (Bryans Garage)

Mr. and Mrs. Randle (Wells Garage)

Mr. Walter Preedy (Ellis Partridge and Co. Ltd.)

Mrs. Gifford

Mr. and Mrs. Cracknell (Thorpe)

The Comrades Club

Messrs A. Field and Son

Mr. F. Stollery

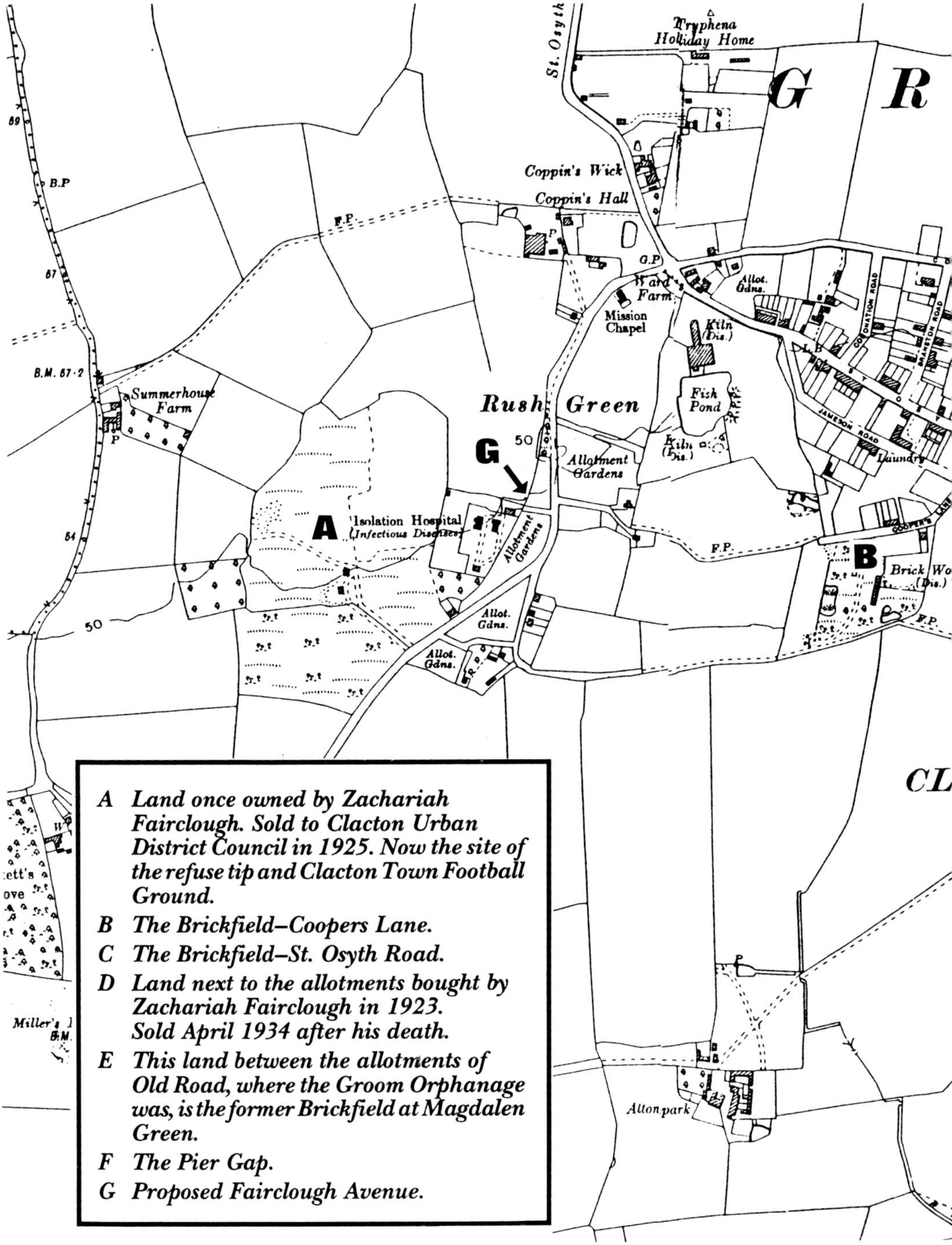

A *Land once owned by Zachariah Fairclough. Sold to Clacton Urban District Council in 1925. Now the site of the refuse tip and Clacton Town Football Ground.*

B *The Brickfield–Coopers Lane.*

C *The Brickfield–St. Osyth Road.*

D *Land next to the allotments bought by Zachariah Fairclough in 1923. Sold April 1934 after his death.*

E *This land between the allotments of Old Road, where the Groom Orphanage was, is the former Brickfield at Magdalen Green.*

F *The Pier Gap.*

G *Proposed Fairclough Avenue.*

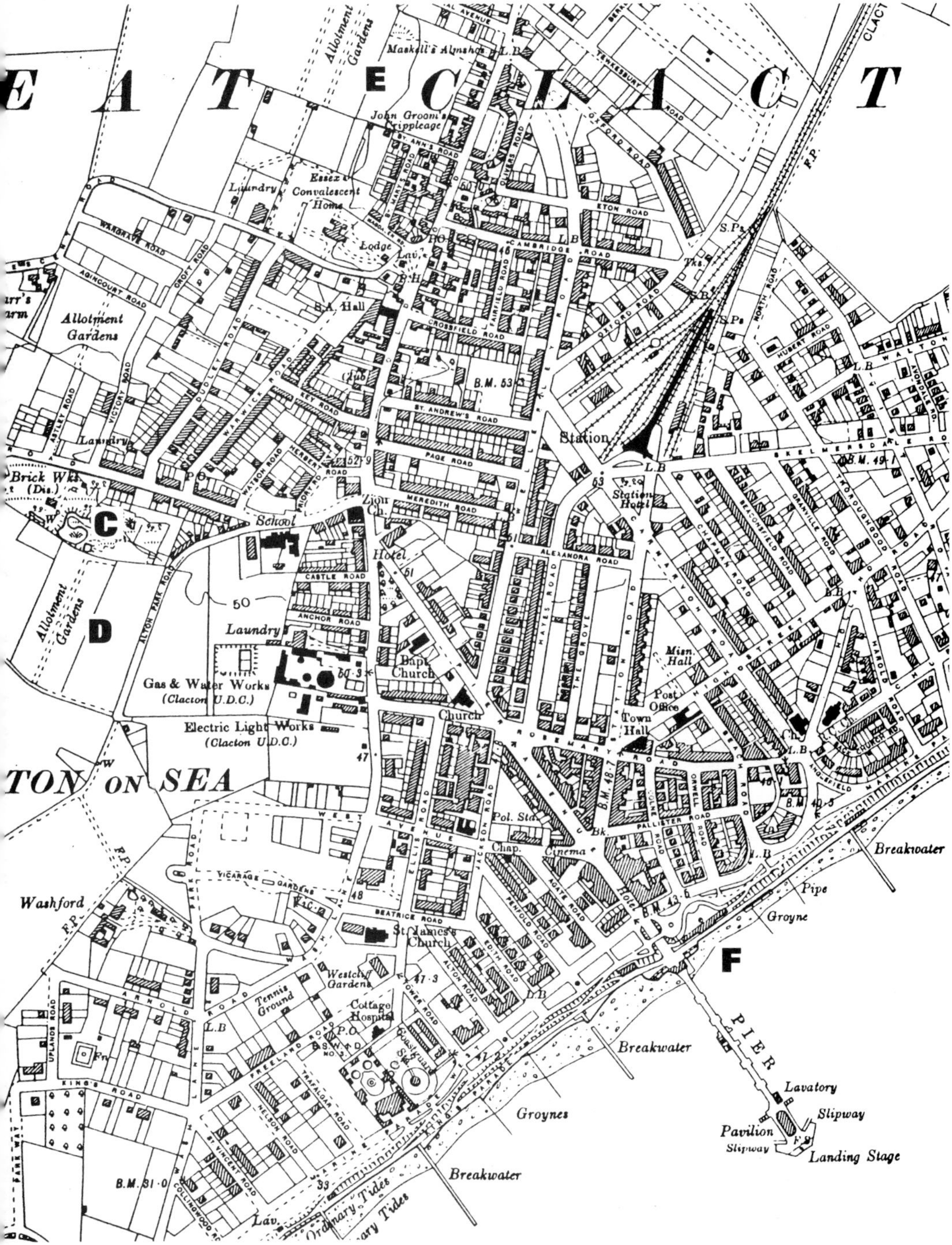
E A T E C L A C T
TON ON SEA
Allotment Gardens
Maskell's Almshos
John Groom's Crippleage
Essex Convalescent Home
Laundry
Lodge
Wargrave Road
Agincourt Road
Croft Road
Tewkesbury Road
Oxford Road
Eton Road
Cambridge Road
St. Ann's Road
Olivers Road
Fairfield Road
Crossfield Road
S.A. Hall
North Road
Hubert Road
Walton Road
Skelmersdale Road
Station
Station Hotel
B.M. 53
St. Andrew's Road
Page Road
Meredith Road
Key Road
Warwick Road
Dudley Road
Victory Road
Astley Road
Watson Road
Herbert Road
Brick Wks. (Dis.)
School
Zion Ch.
Hotel
Castle Road
Anchor Road
Alexandra Road
Hayes Road
The Grove
Station Road
Carnarvon Road
Beaconsfield Road
Chapman Road
Granville Road
Thoroughgood Road
Harold Road
Alton Park Road
Laundry
Gas & Water Works (Clacton U.D.C.)
Electric Light Works (Clacton U.D.C.)
Bapt. Church
Church
Misn. Hall
Post Office
Town Hall
Rosemary Road
High Street
Pier Avenue
Orwell Road
Colne Road
Pallister Road
Pol. Sta.
Chap.
Cinema
Bk.
West Avenue
Ellis Road
Jackson Road
Agate Road
Penfold Road
Vicarage Gardens
Beatrice Road
St. James's Church
Westcliff Gardens
Cottage Hospital
Tennis Ground
Alton Road
Edith Road
Tower Road
Coastguard Stn.
Washford
Arnold Road
Uplands Road
King's Road
Freeland Road
Trafalgar Road
Nelson Road
St. Vincent Road
Collingwood Road
Park Way
Marine Parade
Breakwater
Pipe
Groyne
Groynes
Pier
Lavatory
Slipway
Pavilion
Landing Stage
Ordinary Tides
Lav.
B.M. 31·0
B.M. 48·7
B.M. 43·6
B.M. 40·5
B.M. 49·1
C
D
E
F

BRICKS AND ROLLERS . . .

has been published by the East Anglian Traction Engine Society and is the third book in a series which aims to document previously unrecorded aspects of our agricultural and industrial heritage. By joining the Society you will be helping it to continue this very worthwhile work as well as enjoying for yourself the benefits of a Club which was formed in 1955 (it became a Charitable Society in 1986) to be the focal point of the Steam Preservation movement in East Anglia.

Membership of the Club is open to anyone who has an interest in steam engines and associated artefacts whether an engine owner or not.

Three times a year members receive, free of charge, the Club's Journal 'Steam Preservation' which is one of the most interesting publications available in its category. It contains articles on all aspects of engines, illustrated with photographs both old and new, as well as news on rallies, social items, letters and archival information.

Newsletters are sent out from time to time and the Club runs Social Evenings on a monthly basis, and organises an Annual Dinner.

If you wish to become a member, or find out more about the Club, please contact the Membership Secretary, R. PUMFREY, Springwell Farm, Little Chesterford, Saffron Walden, Essex CB10 1UE. Tel. Saffron Walden 530246.